The Story of Joseph

Middle East Literature in Translation
Michael Beard and Adnan Haydar, *Series Editors*

Other titles in Middle East Literature in Translation

Abundance from the Desert: Classical Arabic Poetry
Raymond Farrin

An Arab's Journey to Colonial Spanish America: The Travels of Elias al-Mûsili in the Seventeenth Century
Elias al-Mûsili; Caesar E. Farah, trans. and ed.

Beyond Love
Hadiya Hussein; Ikram Masmoudi, trans.

Canceled Memories: A Novel
Nazik Saba Yared; Nadine Sinno, trans.

A Muslim Suicide
Bensalem Himmich; Roger Allen, trans.

My Bird
Fariba Vafi; Mahnaz Kousha and Nasrin Jewell, trans.

Thou Shalt Not Speak My Language
Abdelfattah Kilito; Waïl S. Hassan, trans.

Tree of Pearls, Queen of Egypt
Jurji Zaydan; Samah Selim, trans.

The Virgin of Solitude: A Novel
Taghi Modarressi; Nasrin Rahimieh, trans.

The World Through the Eyes of Angels
Mahmoud Saeed; Samuel Salter, Zahra Jishi, and Rafah Abuinnab, trans.

The Story of Joseph

A Fourteenth-Century Turkish Morality Play by Sheyyad Hamza

Translated by

Bill Hickman

Syracuse University Press

This book has been published with the support of the Ministry of Culture and Tourism of Turkey in the framework of the TEDA program.

Syracuse, New York 13244-5290

First Edition 2014

14 15 16 17 18 19 6 5 4 3 2 1

∞ The paper used in this publication meets the minimum requirements of the American National Standard for Information Sciences—Permanence of Paper for Printed Library Materials, ANSI Z39.48-1992.

For a listing of books published and distributed by Syracuse University Press, visit www.SyracuseUniversityPress.syr.edu.

ISBN: 978-0-8156-3357-0 (cloth) 978-0-8156-5270-0 (e-book)

Library of Congress Cataloging-in-Publication Data

Seyyad Hamza, active 13th century, author.

[Yusuf ve Zeliha. English]

The Story of Joseph : a Fourteenth-Century Turkish Morality Play / by Sheyyad Hamza ; translated by Bill Hickman. — First edition.

pages cm. — (Middle East Literature in Translation)

Includes bibliographical references.

ISBN 978-0-8156-3357-0 (cloth : alk. paper) — ISBN 978-0-8156-5270-0 (e-book)

I. Hickman, Bill, translator. II. Title.

PL248.S44Y813 2014

894'.3511—dc23 2013050967

Manufactured in the United States of America

Dedicated to the memory of Peter Molan (1941–2005),
dear friend and stimulating colleague.

Bill Hickman received his PhD from Harvard University. Now retired, he was associate professor of Turkish language and literature in the Department of Near Eastern Studies at the University of California–Berkeley.

Contents

Acknowledgments

I first explored the Old Anatolian Turkish text of Sheyyad Hamza's "Story of Joseph," through a poor photo reproduction of an old manuscript, as a graduate student preparing for comprehensive examinations at Harvard. Twenty years later, teaching at the University of California–Berkeley, I took a much closer look at the text at the request of Michael Chyet, then a graduate student of folklore. Together we read a substantial part of the poem, each bringing his own insights to an always intriguing, sometimes puzzling text.

Shortly after, with the assistance of Tom Walsh in Berkeley's Humanities Computing Service, I entered the text of the poem into a UNIX-based computer on the university campus. With data from the concordance thus generated (using "Key-WordInContext" software), together with a comprehensive word frequency list, I presented papers at annual meetings of the Middle East Studies Association and the American Oriental Society in 1986 and 1987, respectively.

Twenty years later still, now in retirement, Hamza's story intrigued me again. My thought was to publish a comprehensive volume: facing text and translation, copious notes to both, extensive introduction and appendices treating numerous questions and problems. Perhaps I could even resuscitate that massive concordance somehow to show how such data might be useful in studying the text.

Fortunately, common sense prevailed. The realities of scholarly publishing in a field as esoteric as Old Ottoman Turkish literature were grim. Persuaded to read an early brief introduction and sample of the translation, Leslie Peirce (then at Berkeley, now at NYU) encouraged me to pursue a different route: a small volume published by an American university press aimed at university students (in any of a number of disciplines) as well as general readers with a curiosity about Turkish literature, the Middle East, Islam, folklore, or comparative literature. Before long, younger scholars in Turkey produced not one but two new editions of the text, making problematic (if not entirely redundant) any thought I might have had of publishing a "critical edition" of Hamza's poem myself.

So to those who questioned, helped, and encouraged me from the beginning, heartfelt thanks! I would not have come this far without you.

Many others, now over a period of several years, have read parts of the manuscript in much earlier drafts or contributed to my evolving views of Hamza's poem, especially through comments on articles on the same subject. Foremost among them are several former colleagues and old friends: Walter Andrews, Eli Birnbaum, Bob Dankoff, Bill Griswold, Bill Hanaway, Ralph Jaeckel, Gary Leiser, and Karl Zimmer. That I failed to take all of your wise words of advice to heart is a reflection on me and not you. And, as always, errors and omissions are my responsibility alone.

Since our earliest days together as graduate students in Cambridge, Herb Mason has been a steadfast friend, unfailing in his support and encouragement in this and all other undertakings.

The late Kathleen Burrill responded positively when I told her of my publishing plans but did not live long enough to see any of it come to fruition. After her death, her daughter Anne Burrill helped me track down Stephanie Bowie Thomas, whose MA thesis Professor Burrill had directed at Columbia University. Ms. Thomas, in turn, graciously provided me with a copy of that dissertation ("The Story of Joseph in Islamic Literature with an annotated translation of the pre-Ottoman *Destan-i Yusuf* by Şeyyad Hamza"). It is a fine piece of work but appears not to be available in any library in this country, including, regrettably, her own alma mater.

Metin Akar, who wrote an important article on Hamza, generously responded to my long-distance inquiry about more recent work in Turkey on the poem with a long, helpful reply.

Michael Beard took an early interest in my work and facilitated submission of the manuscript to Syracuse.

Alice Kingsnorth gave me timely feedback after reading a section of the translation with a class of students at American River College in Sacramento.

Charles Klopp, among those who first welcomed me to Istanbul before I knew a word of Turkish, read an earlier draft of the entire manuscript and made persuasive suggestions.

James Monroe, former colleague in the Department of Near Eastern Studies at Berkeley, spent several hours helping me understand an *aljamiado* text of the Joseph story.

Many others read and commented on an early draft of the translation: Snejana Akpinar, Marie Boroff, Nancy Eldblom, Marvin Gordon-Lickey, Pat Hickman, Gail Hovey, Bob and Connie Jolly, Rod Kingsnorth, and Vito Victor, to mention those whose names I can still remember.

Several members of a Berkeley book club (Christopher, Effie, Genie, Glen, Kate, Lori, Melissa, and Nina) agreed to read an entire early draft of the translation. They were a helpful test audience. Ian Shepherd, also a member of that book group, went further, commenting on a late draft of the introduction and afterword and providing suggestions on the translation. My thanks to all.

Thanks also to Elissa Mondschein, director of UC–Berkeley's InterLibrary Borrowing Office, and her staff for always courteous, friendly, and prompt help in obtaining difficult to access titles.

The UCB Committee on Research years ago provided me with supplemental funds for early research (including computer time) and small travel grants.

The staff at Syracuse University Press, beginning with Mary Selden Evans (now retired), Suzanne Guiod, Erica Sheftic, and especially Kelly Lynne Balenske, have been patient and forgiving. It has been a pleasure to work with them.

Finally, endless thanks to my wife, Effie Dilworth, my most exacting critic through many drafts, who endured countless discussions and retellings of the Joseph story and who provided invaluable "tech support" at many points along the way. I could not have completed this without her help.

Note on Dating, Spelling, and Reference Works

Unless explicitly noted to the contrary, all dates should be considered "Common Era" (CE) years.

I have anglicized the spelling of a handful of Turkish words, mostly names used repeatedly: so, for example, Sheyyad for Turkish *Şeyyad*. But where I cite, parenthetically, a Turkish word used by Hamza in his poem, I have retained modern Turkish spelling or a more scholarly transcription of his use of the Arabic script, if called for. Those who know the language should be satisfied; others need not be concerned.

Until recently the *Encyclopaedia of Islam*, new edition, was the standard reference work for most matters having to do with the religion, history, and culture of the Islamic world. Intended primarily for scholars, many of its entries are less than suitable for others. Now the *Encyclopaedia of the Qur'an* offers a much more accessible discussion of almost any topic touched on in the Qur'an. For subjects of shared Jewish-Muslim content, the *Encyclopaedia Judaica*, second edition, presents a range of authoritative and accessible articles. For many subjects, all three reference works may be fruitfully searched. Joseph is discussed from a different perspective in each. While the latter two encyclopedias generally use common English forms for their entries, the *Encyclopaedia of Islam* typically uses the Arabic name/word for its entry. In this case, the reader should look for "Yusuf"—found in vol. 11, pp. 352–54. Where I cite articles from these reference works, I use the commonly accepted abbreviations: *EI2*, *EQ*, and *EJ*, respectively.

For citations from the Qur'an and Genesis, I use small roman numerals for sura or chapter numbers and arabic numerals for line (verse). So, for example, Q xii, 32 is Qur'an, sura 12, line 32.

Preface

The Joseph story is one of the most frequently retold tales in world literature. Whether in its archetypal form in the Book of Genesis or its privileged position as a unique complete narrative in sura xii of the Muslim Qur'an, the story gained immense popularity among followers of all three Middle Eastern monotheistic religions. There are hundreds of reformulations of the story based on those two canonical texts. Wherever Jews, Christians, or Muslims went, they took the Joseph story with them and told it again and again.[1]

If modern readers are unfamiliar with the story in either of its sacred book settings, they may well have encountered it—however much transformed—in any of a number of readily accessible, secular reformulations: modern novel, stage play, Broadway musical. It is the story of the despised favorite son who survives the murderous envy of his older brothers. Sold into slavery, he escapes the seductive clutches of his new master's wife and rises to fame and fortune. It is a story with extraordinarily "good legs."

But if it is so well-known, why, one may reasonably ask, should we have yet another retelling of it?

Especially favored for a thousand years by Muslim Turks, from Central Asia to the Balkans, only one of those reformulations has been translated in full and published in English, a volume not readily accessible to the general reader today. Sheyyad Hamza's "Story of Joseph" [*Destan-i Yusuf*], presented here in annotated translation, is a singular cultural document that mimics a particular form of oral storytelling of which nothing else survives. Hamza's poem, a retelling of the story influenced by generations of commentators, embodies and reflects attitudes and beliefs held in fourteenth-century Anatolia in the early years of post-Seljuk, pre-Ottoman rule, and presents its dramatic subject in a different light from that of other reformulations. Hamza's poem is a highly engaging reframing of that ancient story that begs to be told again.

The heart of this book is my translation of Hamza's poem, presented in the form of a stage play, for reasons that are explained in the introduction. Line numbers have been added in the margins, keyed to two recent editions of the Turkish text. There are two reasons for this. It facilitates cross-referencing of points discussed in the introduction. Further, readers with adequate language ability may readily access (in those books) transcriptions of the Old Anatolian Turkish text as well as a modern Turkish rendering and facsimile of the manuscript text. Notes to the translation are intended to elucidate possibly obscure passages, provide reference for quotations, and, less frequently, point readers to further reading.

Works of premodern Turkish literature and the world that they illuminate are relatively unknown outside Turkey. Furthermore, Hamza's poem remains virtually unstudied. Therefore I have provided abundant supporting material in the form of a four-part introduction and an afterword.

The first part of the introduction ("The Story") provides a brief overview of the historical development of the Joseph story up through Hamza's time. "The Poet" (part two) introduces Hamza himself, what little we know of him. In the third part ("Hamza's *Story of Joseph*") I look closely at two extended passages from the text to help the reader better understand Hamza's technique and approach to the story, and offer an overall assessment of the poem. In the final part of the introduction ("The Translation"), I explain my approach to the English version of Hamza's poem.

Readers with little previous experience of Muslim culture or medieval Turkish history should be able to enjoy the story with that introduction. Those who wish for broader background to Hamza's poem will find that in the afterword. It offers answers, I hope, to a variety of questions that a curious reader might ask regarding linguistic, historic, and cultural issues.

Notes to both introduction and afterword refer readers to a wide variety of English language sources for further exploration. They suggest the breadth of writing on matters relating to the Joseph story.

Finally, I provide a synopsis of the entire poem, a list of motifs and incidents identified by line number, to provide access for anyone wishing to compare, at a glance, Hamza's treatment of the story with any other, or simply to quickly find a scene since there are no such divisions in the original poem.

Hamza's text offers numerous points of entry into a study of Islamic culture, especially in its Turkish setting—from its foundational source, the Qur'an, to Anatolian folklore. It is not too much to say, I think, that his "Story of Joseph" could well serve as a subject around which to develop an introduction to the study of Islamic civilization in the premodern Turkish world. I offer Hamza's treatment in the hope that his version will provide non-Turkish readers with a window into his own world and will stimulate interest in Turkish language and culture within the broader context of Islamic civilization.

Notes

1. A subject search for "Joseph, son of Jacob" in the online catalogue of any major library will substantiate the claims. Those results are only the tip of the iceberg.

The Story of Joseph

Introduction

The Story

It begins as the story of the favorite son, envied—no, detested—by his older brothers, a boy who survives their murderous plot and other obstacles, and who rises to great power and reward. If that were all, perhaps the Joseph story would never have achieved the popularity it did.[1] But from the earliest time, an ancient storyteller wove in another story: one of passion and love spurned. Still emotionally incomplete, the story eventually accommodated not one but multiple "returns," each with its own recognition scene, and not one but multiple acts of redemption. In its broadest outline, this is the Joseph story: early exemplary expression of the hero tale, adapted to its ancient Middle Eastern setting.[2]

The boy is Joseph, son of Jacob, great-grandson of Abraham and scion of a line of prophets and patriarchs extending back to Adam; the setting is the land of Canaan.[3] The time is a nearly mythic past—at least several centuries BCE. Joseph is a dreamer, literally. One night he sees himself—as his father interprets it—rising above his brothers to the point of being worshipped by them. Hearing of the dream, the brothers, above all Judah the eldest, plot to do away with him. Through a compromise of sorts, Joseph is dropped into a barren pit—or an actual well, as in our version. A passing caravan camps nearby and Joseph is found and serendipitously rescued, only to be sold as a slave to the traveling merchant by his brothers, who seize an opportunity to rid themselves of their vexatious sibling once and for all (or so they imagine).

Joseph is carried off to Egypt where his new owner resells him, for a handsome profit, to a high official (widely known as the biblical chamberlain Potiphar, in our story as Qutayfar) at the ruler's court. The official's wife is attracted to the (much?) younger Joseph, who seems barely to have reached maturity. He rejects—actually runs away from—the woman's physical advances but pays a heavy price when she turns the tables, accusing him of seducing her. Joseph is imprisoned.

This is the beginning of the story in its oldest surviving form, the first book of the Hebrew Bible (the Old Testament).[4] This Genesis account (chapters 37 and 39–50) framed the Joseph story for Jews, and later Christians, as a further chapter in the history of God's creation of the universe and of the line of Abraham. To that account, subsequent generations of Jewish scholars expanded the story with commentary by way of narrative explanations. Eventually more fantastic details entered in, such as a talking wolf—details we might now call folkloric motifs.[5]

In the early seventh century CE, the Arabian merchant Muhammad was inspired to call his people to believe in and accept one God. The revelations that Muhammad first proclaimed at Mecca and Medina were increasingly accepted as the literal words of God. Gathered together in a collection of chapters (*sura*), this book is the Arabic Qur'an, the foundational source for Muslims. The twelfth chapter, entitled "Yusuf," comprises the story of Joseph. It mirrors the version in Genesis in many essential details.[6]

Subsequent generations of Muslim commentators, like their Jewish predecessors and including prominent early Jewish converts to Islam, added further to the rich lore that embellished the story.[7] The evolving, noncanonical Muslim version of the Joseph story is featured prominently in Arabic language books generally known as "Tales of the Prophets." Prominent examples of this genre are works by Abu Ishak al-Tha'labi and Abu Jafar al-Kisa'i.[8] At the same time, the story became a favored text for popular preachers. (Kisa'i's text is readily understood in that light.)

The oldest surviving freestanding accounts appear to have been written in Persian. Of these, a late eleventh-century adaptation survives that is of disputed authorship and still not adequately studied. It is from this time also that the story came to be well-known as that of "Yusuf and Zulaykha," the latter name now being the one commonly given by Muslim authors to Potiphar's wife. Individual episodes from the Joseph story also figure prominently in the works of seminal Persian Sufi authors from the twelfth and thirteenth centuries, including Attar and Rumi. Mystically oriented exegesis of the Qur'an contributed further to the elaboration of the story with particular emphasis on dreams.[9]

In the biblical story, both Potiphar and his wife vanish not long after the attempted seduction. Later, after Joseph has persuasively interpreted the pharaoh's dream and been freed from prison, he is rewarded with a wife, "Asenath, daughter of

Poti-phera priest of On."[10] Her identity is not further explained in Genesis and her role is primarily to mother Joseph's two sons. However, a "Story of Joseph and Asenath," probably already composed in the first century CE and of disputed Jewish or Christian origin, provided details about her life.[11] Some of those details enlarge on the background of Potiphar's wife and become attached to the woman known as Zulaykha in later Muslim versions of the story. Fleshed out in this way, she becomes a somewhat more fully formed counterpart to the older story's main actor. This enlargement of the story contributed to its blossoming as a romance. It is likely that such narrative development entered the mainstream through works of Judeo-Persian literature, texts written in Persian by Iranian Jews using the Hebrew alphabet.[12]

Mystical imagery and the romantic cast of the story had both became ingrained in popular traditions of the now substantially elaborated tale by the time Turkish-speaking Muslims in Central Asia adopted the Joseph story. Two versions stand out, both written in dialects of Khwarazmian Turkish, the Turkic language then spoken around the Aral Sea. The earliest of these is a verse "Story of Joseph" (Qissa-i Yusuf) by the otherwise obscure 'Ali, from 1233 CE. It is preserved in manuscripts dating only from several centuries later, and no reliable edition of the poem has been published. 'Ali's poem was likely intended for an audience of relatively recent converts to Islam. Nearly a century later, the scholar Nasir al-Din al-Rabghuzi devoted a long section of his "Stories of the Prophets" (Qisas al-Anbiya) to Joseph. His book has both a more literary and a more scholarly character than 'Ali's. Each of these versions proved to be immensely popular, spawning many others.[13]

By the same time the story was being told in Anatolia and by the end of the fourteenth century, several different versions had been written down. ʻAli's version may have had an influence on some of them. Hamza's "Story of Joseph" is one of those which have survived.[14]

Later, better-known versions of the Joseph story, in both Persia and the Ottoman Empire, took a sharp turn to mystical allegory. In the late fifteenth century, Jami's and Hamdullah Hamdi's interpretations, in Persian and Turkish, respectively, became the standards against which—in the Islamic world—almost all other versions came to be measured.[15]

Eventually the story spread to all parts of the world of the originally Near Eastern monotheistic religions.[16] Scenes from Joseph's life were among those prominent in early illustrated Christian Bibles, and those same scenes continued to be favorites for European painters for many centuries. They also provided inspiration to artists working in other media, especially sculptors at work in churches in Europe and elsewhere.[17] Similarly, Muslim painters found such scenes appealing subjects for their miniature illustrations of stories of the Prophets and freestanding versions of the Joseph story (like those of Jami and Hamdi).[18]

In the modern, secular world, the Joseph story gained a new life. Thomas Mann's mid-twentieth-century German novel (*Joseph and His Brothers*), Andrew Lloyd Webber's Broadway musical (*Joseph and the Amazing Technicolor Dreamcoat*), Jason Sherman's Canadian play (*Remnants*), and a verbal riff by the folksinger Arlo Guthrie (on the Zellerbach stage of the University of California, 2008) are just a few among many adaptations.

However the Joseph story is presented, each author, or teller, refashioned it to suit his own purposes. Emphasis may change, even quite drastically. But the themes of jealousy, separation, loss, reunion, forgiveness, and love are predictably present. They are what give the story its extraordinary emotional appeal.

The Poet

"Sheyyad Hamza" is the pen name of one of those fourteenth-century authors of a Turkish-language Joseph story, a poet about whom we know almost nothing. He likely spent at least part of his adult life in the west-central Anatolian city of Akshehir. There in a cemetery is the grave of a young woman who died in 1349, probably of the plague, almost certainly Hamza's daughter. Akshehir (the ancient Philomelion), approximately 100 km northwest of Konya, was probably then under the control of one of the many short-lived Seljuk successor states (*beylik*), either the House of Hamid or the House of Karaman.

Apart from the "Story of Joseph," the name Sheyyad Hamza has been identified with four other, much shorter narrative poems and nearly two dozen short poems—ghazals (Turkish *gazel*)—of simple mystic content. The subject matter of all the poems is consistent and suggests that their author had considerable education and was familiar as well with mystical concepts and their expression in literary figures of speech. In the history of pre-Ottoman and early Ottoman Turkish literature, posthumous attribution of literary works to someone other than the actual author is not uncommon, making the single authorship of the several poems anything but certain. Still, while no analysis of the vocabulary and style of these poems has been attempted, scholars tend to accept them as the work of one and the same person, "Sheyyad Hamza." His "Story of Joseph" is the only one to have received much attention.

"Hamza," a common Muslim name, was almost certainly the poet's own. The word sheyyad (*şeyyad*), however, is of obscure origin (Persian or Arabic) and not well attested. The word loosely denoted a public teller of tales who spoke or narrated in a loud voice, and it did not survive the sixteenth century. At least one other poet contemporary with Hamza was similarly nicknamed, but the actual practice of the sheyyad is not well explained in contemporary sources. (Another meaning of the word was someone who worked as a plasterer.) As we shall see, the poem's narrator sounds like what we might expect of a professional storyteller, or sheyyad. It may be debated whether Hamza himself was a sheyyad; perhaps the pen name is only a literary conceit. But Hamza's narrator, his alter ego so to speak, and whom we may identify with "Sheyyad Hamza," is key to an appreciation of the poem. In what follows, I refer to the poet only by the name Hamza. Consistent with the character of his narrator, I will generally speak of Hamza's audience or his listeners, not his readers.

In historical perspective, Hamza lived at roughly the same time as the renowned North African traveler Ibn Battuta, whose route through Anatolia took him close to but not actually through Akshehir.[19] Hamza would also have been a close contemporary of the highly regarded, and much better known, Turkish mystic poet Yunus Emre.[20] Hamza's poem was probably composed midway through the century bracketed by Dante's *Divine Comedy* and Chaucer's *Canterbury Tales*. A coincidence, certainly, but of interest nonetheless is the fact that an anonymous "Joseph and Jacob" was written in Middle English not long before Hamza's story.[21]

Hamza's "Story of Joseph"

"Listen to the words of this tale I shall tell you. I will relate the story of Joseph—how it happened. I worked day and night to put it all into verse. The beauty of the story will wipe away all the cares from the heart of any listener. Of all the writings in the pages of the Qur'an, this is the most beautiful of stories."

With these words, Hamza introduces his version of the story to his fourteenth-century Anatolian audience. Thus he relates his poem to the foundational Muslim version of the Joseph story.[22] Even as he embellishes it with numerous motifs, narrative twists, and entire backstories, Hamza takes sura xii as an inspirational source for his own tale, briefly quoting its Arabic text (and phrases from other suras) in a dozen verses and paraphrasing it in numerous other lines. He will explicate it and elaborate upon it for maximum rhetorical effect.

Before he begins the story proper, Hamza quotes the Arabic phrase *bismillah* ("In the name of God"), the first words of the Qur'an, with which all beginnings are entered upon. He goes on to invoke several of the most common of those "names," including the two, the Merciful (*al-Rahim*) and the Compassionate (*al-Rahman*), that follow after the *bismillah* in the Qur'an, words that would have been familiar to every Anatolian Turk, however casually a follower of Islam.

Hamza then invokes blessings on the prophet Muhammad and offers greetings to the "imams," prayer leaders, but here more specifically the first four "rightly guided" caliphs who succeeded to leadership of the Muslim community after Muhammad's death (632 CE).[23]

Dispensing with any sort of dedication or statement explaining how he came to compose his poem, points that a more self-conscious poet would normally have included, and having three times referred to the story as "sweet," Hamza now launches into his tale.

To get a sense of Hamza's narrative style and to clear up some potentially confusing matters, consider the following summaries of two extended passages. Each constitutes a major digression with details probably unfamiliar even to readers conversant with the Joseph story in any of its other versions. Call the first of these "The Well."

The Well (ll. 0100–194)

At this point in his story, Hamza has introduced the prophet Jacob and his family. Joseph has ten older brothers. He and his one younger brother, Benjamin, are the sons of Rachel, now dead.[24] Hamza has related one of Joseph's dreams (and explained Jacob's interpretation of future greatness) and revealed his brothers' jealousy. Having connived to take Joseph away from their father and do away with him, the brothers have reached the scene of their crime and have put a rope around Joseph. So: "The well is deep. They cut the rope so [Joseph] would fall" (l. 0101).

At that moment of dramatic suspense, "A command came to Gabriel . . . Do not let Joseph fall! . . . Gabriel came to Earth [and] caught hold of Joseph."[25]

Allowing the listener barely a moment to catch his breath, Hamza's narrator digresses: "Now here there is a break in the story. I will describe that well to you, tell you who dug it" (l. 0105).[26] In the following lines, we are quickly introduced to the pre-Islamic Arabian ruler Sheddad, son of Ad, and to Hud, figures well-known from the Qur'an. Hud, one of the non-biblical Arabian prophets, was a steadfast reader, we are told, of one of the sacred books associated with Seth, third son of Adam. In that book, Hud had read about (the yet unborn) Joseph and his extraordinary beauty. Desiring to see Joseph's face, Hud was instructed to go down into Sheddad's well and wait, which he did—for 1,200 years![27]

At this moment, Joseph (reappearing now in the narrative) dramatically appears to Hud. His desire satisfied, Hud expires peacefully, but not before telling Joseph, "Know your travails come from God . . . This trouble . . . is because of Him. Now prostrate yourself before God" (ll. 0122–23).

Here Gabriel reenters the narrative and reassures Joseph with a prophecy: "You will exercise great authority in the world" (l. 0126). With that the narrator announces, "I have come back to my story" (l. 0128). Leaving Joseph in the well, he now describes the treacherous acts of Joseph's brothers. Returned home, having presumably eliminated Joseph, they lie to their father, concocting a story about the boy's disappearance. Jacob's sorrow at the loss of his adored son, hinted at in his earlier reluctance to let Joseph out of his sight, knows no bounds. It becomes one of the story's powerful themes.

Here Hamza's narrator, again abruptly, returns to his earlier digression: "Listen, there is more" (l. 0165). He introduces a merchant from Egypt who, in a dream, sees himself "in Canaan in the Well of Ad"—that is, in the same well into which Joseph was dropped. An interpreter interprets the merchant's dream favorably and advises him to go to the site of the dream, which he does. But there the merchant is summarily told to "come back in fifty years and look again."[28] In what seems like the blink of an eye, fifty years have passed and the merchant is at the well again, his slaves poised to drop a bucket down for water. The narrator has brought us back, once again, to where he had left us a few lines earlier. "At that moment Gabriel came and greeted Joseph," advising him to "prepare to rise up out of the well" (ll. 0189–91).

Whether—after this prolonged digression with its leaps of time and space (and another within it)—we are ready for the main narrative to resume (which it now does), there is a great deal to be astonished at here. In this extended passage, Hamza masterfully (or shamelessly) manipulates his audience's attention with these sudden changes of narrative course. The introduction of this two-part backstory (who dug the well and how the Egyptian merchant, who will soon purchase Joseph, came to be there) distracts our attention and delays our awareness of Joseph's fate. These two secondary "well scenes" ripple out from the central plot's main event and reinforce the drama. They also give Hamza an opportunity to introduce another dream (and its interpretation) into his story. "Patience!" Hamza seems to say to us. And, implicitly, to Jacob as well.

The second digression is briefer and less complicated. It provides a balancing introduction for the character who will occupy center stage, with Joseph, on into the second half of the poem.

Zeliha, Daughter of Taymus (ll. 0326–76)

Neither the Bible nor the Qur'an offers any explanation as to how Zeliha came to be the wife of the high chamberlain ("Potiphar" in Genesis and "Qutayfar" in Hamza's poem; unnamed in the Qur'an) at the Egyptian court. In the canonical texts, she does not have a name of her own. Hamza provides a brief explanation of who she is. "Zeliha was the daughter of the Lord of the West. His name was Taymus . . . One night . . . (she) saw the image of a man. That image was Joseph's."[29] Zeliha's dreams multiply. She falls hopelessly in love with the image; her desire pushes her toward madness. In Zeliha's third dream, the image tells her, "I am that mighty one of Egypt. Come . . . find me and see who I am" (l. 0343).

Willing to do anything to help his daughter and taking that "mighty one" to be the ruler of Egypt, Taymus sends him a letter. In short order, Zeliha travels to Egypt to be the mighty one's bride. But she soon discovers that Qutayfar is *not* the man of her dreams.

Joseph by now has been brought to Egypt by the merchant. He will be auctioned off to the highest bidder. At this point in the narrative, where Hamza has nearly brought Zeliha and the real man of her dreams together, the story moves forward. Zeliha's attempted seduction of Joseph, and its disastrous consequences for him that follow, are essential to the Qur'an's narrative, and they will not be ignored by Hamza. He plays the story for all it's worth. Zeliha's passion for Joseph will know no limits, but, as in the Qur'an, their "relationship" ultimately remains secondary.

In later Muslim literature, the Joseph story is often named and told as "(The Story of) Joseph and Zeliha" in which Zeliha's love for Joseph, paragon of beauty, becomes the center of an allegorical tale: the love of the mystic for God. In his poem, Hamza employs some of the familiar imagery of such mystic poetry: the unbearable pain of separation from the beloved leading to deathly sickness (ll. 0331–46 and 0448ff), sight of the beloved's face as life-giving sustenance (ll. 0319), the withering sigh of the lover powerful enough to set objects on fire (ll. 0899–900), and branding the heart with the fire of longing to increase one's suffering (l. 1086). At one point, Hamza briefly presents Joseph himself as a sufi going off to his own private meditation cell (*halvethane*; l. 1108).[30]

Hamza's elaboration of sura xii is less about mystical love, however, than about trust in God, an essential message of the Qur'an itself. At the end of what I have called the "Well" scene and immediately after Gabriel advises Joseph to prepare to leave the well, Hamza reveals the direction of his own story: "See how timely this story comes to us. Now Joseph had looked into the mirror, had seen his own appearance and was amazed. Joseph: 'How beautifully God created me.'"[31] As Hamza's narrator says, commenting on Joseph's exclamations, "These were the words which brought catastrophe on Joseph" (ll. 0192–94).

Joseph is certainly handsome: "a beautiful boy, like no other" (l. 0020), as beautiful even as the houris with "a face as beautiful as the full moon" (l. 0199). Recall that Hud was willing to wait 1,200 years for a sight of that face. But above all, it is Joseph's pride in his beauty that Hamza singles out as the root cause of his tribulations. His vanity prevents Joseph from recognizing who controls man's actions. So, later in the poem, with the following questions Gabriel brings Joseph up short, challenging him to recognize God's omnipotence as Joseph's essential powerlessness: "Joseph, tell me, who caused Jacob to love you? . . . And who saved you from your brothers? . . . And who removed you from the well? . . . Who shielded you from that woman, Zeliha?" (ll. 0647–51).

Joseph's overweening pride is something Gabriel must repeatedly warn him against and for which Joseph must repeatedly seek pardon from God. Pride is Joseph's principal moral failing, nearly his undoing. It is what distracts him from keeping his trust in God. If one wishes to impute mystical inspiration to Hamza's poem, we might find that in his preoccupation with a fundamental task of the would-be sufi: the overcoming of base human impulses, and chief among them pride.[32]

The Sheyyad

Hamza's story survives today in a unique, handwritten copy from the sixteenth century. Its compositional form is a poem of 1,528 couplets, each consisting of a pair of end-rhyming half lines. This poetic form (*mesnevi*) was used in his time for long narrative subjects. As noted above, Hamza followed, if only very loosely, certain conventional practices at the beginning of his poem—remembrance and praise of the One God and Muhammad. He may also have used one of the Perso-Arab meters for his poem, though this is debated.[33]

However much, or little, Hamza adopted literary forms, his poem has many characteristics of a performance narrated by an actor speaking throughout in the first person, before a live audience. In frequent, brief asides, Hamza's narrator urges those gathered in his presence to pay attention, to "listen up"; he comments on—and now and then explains—actions that he has just narrated; he wheedles and implores his listeners, prods them to offer prayers for Muhammad. He even self-consciously remarks on his own storytelling skills.[34] Sometimes it is difficult to tell when Hamza's narrator pauses to address his audience (and us) and when the narrative of his story continues. There is a nearly seamless flow.[35] The narrator is not so much a character *in* Hamza's story as he is the ever-present, highly engaged teller of it.

Assuming the persona of the popular, perhaps itinerant preacher, Hamza's narrator is at his fiery best in a series of five mini-sermons (*nükte*) interspersed throughout the tale and ranging in length from six to fifty-nine lines.[36] Each is prompted by an incident in the story to which it relates. Each in turn relates a situation at the Day of Resurrection, emphasizing the total servitude of man to God. The Devil, "that accursed one," has a role to play in these eschatological dramas but he will be outmaneuvered in the end. The Prophet Muhammad will make his intercession available to true believers. The moral of each of these short lessons is adherence to the "straight path" (*togrı yol*; l. 1481), yet another quotation, by translation, from the Qur'an's opening sura (Q i, 6).[37]

While there is a long, richly documented tradition of oral storytelling among Turkish-speaking peoples, especially the minstrel bard accompanying himself on a stringed instrument, the specific art of the fourteenth-century Anatolian Turkish sheyyad is undocumented.[38] A later tradition of storytellers named *meddahs* is recorded, and those sound (on the page at least) something like our imagined sheyyad.[39] Whether the sheyyad filled a slightly different storytelling role, narrated a story of a different subject, or merely, in some sense, evolved into the meddah, are probably moot points, beyond knowing. Nor are we likely to know whether Hamza himself ever shouted out his story "in a loud voice," or entertained, or even preached to an audience. Hamza's poem may be the closest we get to a record of an actual sheyyad's performance.

How Hamza's poem came to be first written down—a text now lost to us—and for whom and for what purpose (to be read? to be used as a sort of prompt text?) are also questions for which we will probably never have answers. The sole surviving copy of that manuscript—written two centuries after the poem's composition—has suffered from scribal intervention, intentional and unintentional.[40] Yet it seems clear to me—and I hope readers will soon have reason to agree—that his poem, however much Hamza says he labored over it, conveys an air of authentic live, spoken performance. So here is an inescapable contradiction: the essentially orally imagined and delivered story set down and preserved on the (now printed) page.

We have already seen how Hamza's poem is rooted in the Qur'an. He makes passing reference also to matters with which a Muslim of even nominal religious training would have been familiar: the pre-eternal pen and tablet (ll. 0323 and 0483); paradise and the houris believed to await true believers there (l. 0008); Azra'il, the Angel of Death (ll. 1212 and 1447); and the Day of Judgment and the final torments of the devil (see note

37). For his Turkish audience, these would likely have required little explanation.[41]

Hamza's narrative derives from a multilayered tradition of commentary and the creative imaginations of many inspired storytellers. Disentangling those contributions, one from another, would be a daunting task—probably an impossible one. Some motifs have entered the narrative, whatever Hamza's immediate source, from anecdotes related in stories told about other prophets. So, for example, Joseph's powerfully whinnying horse (ll. 0857ff.) recalls a similar steed owned by Seth, a gift from his father, Adam. Seth too is said to have been the object of an attempted seduction (by the Devil). Recalling that Hud reads a Book of Seth while waiting to see Joseph in the Well of Ad, we may see a virtual cluster of details around this ancient figure, explicit and implicit, that have found their way into some versions of the Muslim Joseph story.[42] But who can say exactly how such material combines over time?

Hamza's story world is vividly animated by popular belief, notions well outside the range of the Qur'an's spare text. So, for example, Gabriel is shown appearing as a bird (l. 0409), Joseph's skills at dream interpretation have their origin in a white stone placed in his mouth (l. 0615),[43] Zeliha's virginity is protected by a fairy and her youth is restored by Gabriel (ll. 0367 and 0916).[44]

Hamza's narrative has numerous touches of realism—a palace "all roofs and chimneys" (l. 0304); a load described as "fit for a camel," not a mule (l. 0957); a sleeve held modestly up before a face (l. 0724); a bead pinned to a child's clothing, presumably to ward off the evil eye (l. 1155). But just as often, his imagery suggests the fabulous aspects of the fairy tale: a cup's magical ring, when struck, can be understood by Joseph (ll. 1281 f.), and a magic bracelet moves from arm to arm of its own accord (l. 1053). Other features of Hamza's poem are consistent with this overall "feel" of the narrative.

Apart from adopting a generally hyperbolic tone, Hamza uses rounded-off and especially large numbers for hyperbolic effect. Joseph's worth as a slave is said to be more than 5,000 pieces of gold (l. 0382); a bracelet is worth, variously, 10,000 or 12,000 Egyptian gold pieces (ll. 0679 and 1043); God grants the merchant "forty sons" upon Joseph's prayer (l. 0401). Elsewhere, however, Hamza occasionally uses an oddly precise figure (so at l. 1405, "seventy-three days") where none seems called for. In such instances, he may be filling out a line for better metrical effect.

The sense of time, as we have seen, is also fantastic. Apart from examples noted above, Jacob wonders whether he will have to wait "seventy years" (or perhaps only forty) before he will see Joseph again (ll. 0134–36). Long journeys are accomplished in the briefest of times. Hamza uses the expression "to make a long story short" (*söz öküşdür*; literally, "words are many") to communicate his compression of time and an absence of detail (ll. 0178, 0301, and elsewhere). Joseph's brothers make the trip between Canaan and Egypt in the space between two couplets (ll. 1396 and 1397); Zeliha draws pictures of herself and Joseph on new palace walls seemingly before they have even been constructed (l. 0480).

Hamza's story is also marked by frequent narrative inconsistency. Thus, prisoners remain incarcerated even after the ruler has freed them (ll. 0611 and 0752); Joseph asks his Arab visitor where he is from despite having just been told (ll. 0663–68); grain grows even when none has been planted (ll. 0829–30).

Some such "slips of the tongue" may be explained by scribal error. But the number and egregiousness of these "mistakes" point not to a careless copyist but rather to their origin in the presumed oral culture of Hamza's storytelling world.

More disconcerting, perhaps, the roles of the pharaoh and his chamberlain (and their relationship) seem confused. This is largely due to the Qur'anic narrative that introduces only a single ruler, the unnamed "king" (*malik*), husband of the woman who will attempt to seduce Joseph. In Hamza's telling, the presumed subordinate, Qutayfar, is referred to as "sultan" while the man he presumably serves is the king, "[Malik] Reyyan." The latter enters the story abruptly (l. 0603), and when Qutayfar sickens and dies he is oddly succeeded by the king—strangely now said to be Qutayfar's brother (ll. 0609–10).[45] The entry of Jewish lore into Muslim traditions of the Joseph story partly explains the resulting complexity but also inadvertently adds to it, at least in Hamza's telling.

Inadvertence aside, there is a single passage in Hamza's tale that strikes me as odd. In an effort to remedy Zeliha's lovesickness that a doctor has failed to cure, the narrator introduces a nurse. In the longest section of uninterrupted speech in the entire poem (ll. 0461–75), this presumably modest woman suggests that Zeliha have architects build her a fine palace of sumptuous rooms, ornately decorated, and, as a final touch, with suggestively painted scenes of Zeliha and Joseph placed throughout. The passage is notable for a high incidence of Arabic and Persian terms for jewels and precious stones, words that

Hamza's listener would not likely have understood. How to explain this strange intrusion?

While it is plausible that a copyist added such a lengthy passage to the poem, it is more likely that the nurse's words were borrowed by Hamza from some older written source. But why he included this singularly incongruous "speech" to his generally lively, fast-moving story is a mystery to me. It remains truly a narrative inconsistency.

Finally, for a Western reader familiar with the biblical (or the Qur'anic) story, one of the striking features of Hamza's poem is a certain transformation of the historical landscape. Hamza intends the story to appeal to his audience through a subtle—but to our ears perhaps strange—time warp. Hamza gives his audience no pharaohs or pyramids. Pointedly he tells us that Zeliha's father, Taymus, "worshipped the cross. That Christian wasted his life for nothing at all." This may strike us as jarringly anachronistic—there were no Christians in pharaonic Egypt. But for Hamza, in a country (Anatolia) where Muslims were likely still a minority, and where tensions between Muslim and Christians may have still run high, it made sense to fill his narrative landscape with people of a recognizable faith.[46] Readers will also note that on the merchant's travels to Egypt with Joseph in tow, he passed through a number of Canaanite cities ruled by idol-worshipping kings (ll. 0257–89). These may suggest biblical figures, or even idolators from Muhammad's own Arabia, but to an audience from Hamza's century they would more likely have appeared as Christian rulers.

Hamza introduces Jacob (l. 0018), appropriately, as a prophet (*peygamber*), and Joseph is acknowledged as obtaining the same distinction following Jacob's death (l. 1476). Readers may be surprised, however, when Joseph's brothers speaking to their father (earlier, l. 1006) refer to Joseph's religion as Islam. This is in keeping with the Muslim view that genuine submission to the One God (*islam*) was the true religion of Abraham and successive prophets. So when Joseph is formally called to prophethood, he invites the people of Egypt to the "true faith," that is, Islam. Because the Egyptians refused to give up their religious ways, Joseph "destroyed the churches, smashed their crosses" (l. 1477) in a fit of anger. Rather than any historically precise, pre-Christian Egypt, then, Hamza's setting for Joseph's actions recalls a landscape familiar to his Anatolian compatriots.[47]

In a perceptive essay, Anthony Johns has written that in order to appreciate sura xii, one must be attuned to "the rhetorical idiom in which the story is told . . . Essentially, the Qur'anic presentation of the story is to *be heard*." And he goes on to describe the sura as "a rapidly moving series of scenes, *something like a morality play*."[48]

It would be blasphemous to a Muslim for any other version of the Joseph story to be put on par with sura xii. But Johns's assessments are applicable to Hamza's telling of the story as well. His is also essentially "a morality play . . . to be heard."

Following his many predecessors, Hamza opens up, expands, and interprets the story's canonical source. Descriptions are provided, dialogue created. Indeed, reading Hamza's poem today we are struck by how he achieves his dramatic goal. At those points where we might expect elaboration for maximum emotional effect, we have just the opposite. For example, Joseph's pardoning of his brothers (l. 1321), echoed in

Jacob's similar pardoning of them (l. 1401), is accomplished in a single declarative sentence of two words. The drama is all in the lines leading up to these moments and in the repetition of words to communicate that buildup—all the weeping and tears, the fainting and falling down, and the rising up again. Hamza's technique may be partly the result of the relatively unsophisticated language at his disposal—from the point of view of the later development of Ottoman Turkish. But that technique resonates with long-established practices of Turkish oral storytelling.

However sura xii is interpreted—and readers will have different responses—it is, as Johns says, as much as anything "the story of a father whose son is lost and then found." What dominates the Qur'an's narrative, in his view, is "Jacob's grief at losing Joseph, a grief compounded by the fear that he has lost also Benjamin." So in Hamza's poem, Jacob's apprehension of his imminent loss of Joseph and his grief following his actual loss are present at the beginning and powerfully echoed and reintroduced as the story nears its end. If word frequency seems an unlikely indicator of an author's purpose, it is the case that in Hamza's text Jacob's name occurs more frequently than any other except Joseph's. In the telling of the Joseph story, many authors, and commentators, have concentrated on the relationship between Zeliha and Joseph. But while in Hamza's story Zeliha (briefly) outlives Jacob, it is his long suffering that weighs more heavily in the end.[49]

Hamza's Turkish audience in Akshehir would hardly have understood the Qur'an's Arabic text of the Joseph story, with its inspired complexity. But what better way to convey the drama and the lessons of the sura for those listeners than a paraphrase, delivered forte, in their own language. Hamza surely imagined he could achieve that end with his one-man performance.

The Translation

Hamza's language is a mostly simple and straightforward Turkish, albeit from the fourteenth century, befitting his fictional narrator addressing an imagined audience in an oral performance. I have attempted to match his language with simple and straightforward English.

It might have been possible to rephrase Hamza's lines into some sort of rhyming or metered English verse. But I am not a poet and that approach would have led to a patently bad outcome, inauthentic and unsatisfying in every way. I have tried to let the natural rhythms of my own language animate the translation. Throughout I have kept the translation as close to Hamza's Turkish as seemed appropriate.

Despite Hamza's choice of form—a poem of rhyming couplets with fixed meter—the spirit of his narrative calls for a different strategy in translation, as I have argued above. Therefore I have taken the liberty to format his poem as a play. This has required mainly a simple change in the presentation of Hamza's text. Where a line of his poem begins: "Joseph says . . ." followed by another, "Zeliha says . . ." I have substituted the speakers' names, followed by their actual speech, doing away altogether with the repetitious and unnecessary "he said . . . she said." This alteration involves no other change in the translation, nor any change in the meaning of the lines.

I have highlighted the narrator's frequent asides, interjections, and digressions—words specifically addressed to his audience, not part of the story proper—with italics.

I have, however, suppressed another interjection: line-ending nouns—for example, the words *uya* ("brother"), *hoca* ("sir, master"), *yara* ("oh friend")—with which Hamza often fills out a line metrically, words that provide necessary rhyme.[50] These words are arbitrary, add nothing of meaning to Hamza's poem, and may become annoying to the modern reader. There is enough repetition already in the text to warrant the jettisoning of them without any serious loss of effect.

Hamza repeatedly switches back and forth between past and continuous present verb tenses. Use of the latter (aorist) tense adds to the prevailing sense of immediacy of his storyteller's narration. It may also be that the poet uses it merely to lengthen an otherwise short syllable. I have felt free to use both tenses, rather arbitrarily, in my translation.

The reader of Hamza's Turkish poem, I imagine, will be struck by the abundance of verbs—sometimes as many as six in a single couplet. This creates a strong sense of action and movement that gives the narrative its particular character—to me a frequently breathless quality. To my own (foreign) ear, this terse, clipped approach creates a sense of urgency that would have produced the appropriate effect. Does the same situation occur in translation? The reader will have to judge.

Apart from narrative inconsistencies, as noted above, here and there the reading of the sixteenth-century copy of Hamza's text remains opaque: likely copyist error concealing obscure original wording. In such cases, I have used my best judgment to produce a plausible rendering.

Notes to the translation, despite my best efforts, are more numerous than I would like. At the end of each note, I add in parentheses the line number of the Turkish text in order that readers who so desire can find the passage in question in either of the two recent reeditions of the poem.[51] Others may ignore them.

To call the hero of the tale "Joseph" or "Yusuf"? It seemed wisest, in the end, to retain the name best known in English and so also to avoid inconsistency as much as possible elsewhere. Would readers have been as comfortable with Yakub, Rubil, and Yahuda? I thought not. On the other hand, I have retained "Qutayfar" as it seems no more foreign than Potiphar. "Zeliha," variant of Zuleyha, may also be unfamiliar to English speakers, but the name has no common Anglicized form so choice was not an issue. I have retained as well other names that have no English counterparts at all, for example, Mamil.

Hamza calls God by many different names, among them *hak*, *sultan*, *rab*, *çalab*, *padişah*, *tanrı*, and, less frequently, *allah*. In most instances, it seemed best to retain simply "God." He uses also, besides *rahim* and *rahman*, several of the Arabic "names" of God, terms that I have translated with straightforward English equivalents—"the Pardoner" (*gufran*; l. 0003), "the Generous" (*kerim*; 0007), and "the Everpresent" (*hazır*; 0442), among others.

Notes

1. I use the expression "Joseph story" (but without quotation marks) to refer broadly to the story outlined here but not any unique version of it.

2. My sketch of the story's development here should be read suggestively, not as literal explanation of how the Joseph story evolved. For an

outline of the hero story, see Lord Raglan, "The Hero of Tradition, in Robert A. Segal, ed., *The Myth and Ritual Theory: An Anthology* (Malden, MA: Blackwell, 1998), 193–208. By "return," I refer to the reuniting of the hero with a loved one from whom he has been long separated.

3. Biblical Canaan is roughly coterminous with Israel and the Palestinian West Bank.

4. For the Bible's first book: Robert Alter, trans., *Genesis* (W. W. Norton: New York, 1996). The Egyptian story of Anubis and Bata includes an attempted seduction that likely finds an echo in the Genesis account. See Susan Hollis, *The Ancient Egyptian "Tale of Two Brothers,"* 2nd ed. (Oakville CT: Bannerstone Press, 2008).

5. For one interpretation of the expansion of material comprising the Hebrew Joseph story, see James L. Kugel, *In Potiphar's House: The Interpretive Life of Biblical Texts* (New York: Harper, 1990). Jewish stories about Joseph were published by Louis Ginzberg as part of his monumental *The Legends of the Jews*, trans. Henrietta Szold (Baltimore: Johns Hopkins University Press, 1998), 2: 3–184. In a foreword to volume 1, Kugel describes Ginzberg's work as an assemblage of "many fanciful elaborations and embellishments of biblical stories . . . [retold] as one continuous narrative" (ix).

6. The translation of Marmaduke Pickthall, *The Meaning of the Glorious Quran* has long standing as a reliable English text. Less well-known but suggestive is the "rendering" of Anthony H. Johns in his "Joseph in the Qur'an: Dramatic Dialogue, Human Emotion, and Prophetic Wisdom," *Islamochristiana* 7 (1981): 44–55.

7. The character of Muslim exegesis is illustrated by A.F.L. Beeston, *Baidawi's Commentary on Surah 12 of the Qur'an* (Oxford: Oxford University Press, 1963). Explicitly Jewish material that entered the mainstream of Muslim narratives is generally known as *Isra'iliyyat*.

8. See, respectively, William M. Brinner, trans., *Lives of the Prophets as recounted by Abu Ishaq Ahmad ibn Muhammad ibn Ibrahim al-Tha'labi* (Boston: Brill, 2002), hereafter *Tha'labi*; and W. M. Thackston Jr., *The Tales of the Prophets of al-Kisa'i* (Boston: G. K. Hall, 1978), hereafter *Kisa'i*. Thackston's introduction (xi–xxxiv) includes a more detailed overview of the growth of the tradition of prophet tales.

9. The name Zulaykha sometimes takes the form "Zeliha," as in Hamza's poem. For mystical exegesis of the Qur'an, see Mohammad J. Mahallati, "The Significance of Dreams and Dream Interpretation in the Qur'an: Two Sufi Commentaries on Surat Yusuf," in Louise Marlow, ed., *Dreaming across Boundaries: The Interpretation of Dreams in Islamic Lands* (Boston: Ilex Foundation, 2008), 153–78. For more on Attar, see below, n. 30. For Rumi, see the afterword, n. 17.

10. At Genesis xli, 50.

11. For a concise overview, see Noegel and Wheeler, *Historical Dictionary of Prophets in Islam and Judaism* (Lanham, MD: Scarecrow Press, 2002), 176 ("Joseph and Asenath"). A detailed study of the story is Ross Shepard Kraemer, *When Aseneth Met Joseph* (New York: Oxford University Press, 1998).

12. In his retelling of the Book of Genesis, the Judeo-Persian "Bereshit-namah," Mowlana Shahin-i Shirazi, a close contemporary of Hamza's, presents his own version of the Joseph story. See Vera Basch Moreen, *In Queen Esther's Garden: An Anthology of Judeo-Persian Literature* (New Haven: Yale University Press, 2000), 26–31 and 38–55 (for an English translation of the section, "Jacob and the Wolf").

13. For the first, see Steven L. West, "The First Story of Joseph in Turkic Islamic Literature" (PhD diss., UCLA, 1975); for the second, H. E. Boeschoten, J. O'Kane, and M. Vandamme, trans., *Al-Rabghuzi: The Stories of the Prophets*, vol. 2 (Leiden: Brill, 1995), 163–279.

14. Roughly contemporary with Hamza's "Story" is an anonymous Arabic poem of similarly popular style but lacking any trace of a narrator. See R. Y. Ebied and M.J.L. Young, *The Story of Joseph in Arabic Verse: The Leeds Arabic Manuscript 347* (Leiden: Brill, 1975). This should be read in conjunction with the cautionary review by A.F.L. Beeston, "Notes on a Middle Arabic 'Joseph' Poem," *Bulletin of the School of Oriental and African Studies* 40 (1977): 287–96.

15. An abridged translation of Jami's poem is David Pendlebury, *Yusuf and Zulaikha: An Allegorical Romance by Hakim Nuruddin Abdurrahman Jami* (London: Octagon Press, 1980). A summary of Hamdi's poem and selections from it are given by E.J.W. Gibb, *A History of Ottoman Poetry*, vol. 2, ed. E. G. Browne (London: Luzac, 1965), 142–72.

16. For English translations of Muslim Joseph story texts from Chinese Turkestan (a single scene) and Kenya, see Gunnar Jarring, *Literary Texts from Kashgar* (Lund, 1980), 46–55; and Jan Knappert, *Islamic Legends: Histories of the Heroes, Saints, and Prophets of Islam*, (Leiden: E. J. Brill, 1985), 85–104, respectively. For a discussion of the Joseph story in Javanese Muslim literature, see M. C. Ricklefs, *The Seen and Unseen Worlds in Java, 1726–1749* (Honolulu: University of Hawai'i Press, 1998), 53–61. For a Christian version from Africa, E. Isaac, "The Ethiopic History of Joseph," *Journal for the Study of the Pseudepigrapha* 6 (1990): 3–125. For English versions of seven texts from Spain, reflecting Jewish, Christian, and Muslim sensibilities: Michael McGaha, *Coat of Many Cultures* (Philadelphia: Jewish Publication Society, 1997). When Albanian Muslims began writing in their own language (in the Arabic script), one of the earliest creations was a version of the Joseph story by the poet Muhamet Kyçyku. For details, see Robert Elsie, *History of Albanian Literature* (Boulder, CO: Social Science Monographs, 1995), 1: 107–11.

17. For illustrations of the Joseph story from early Christian Bibles, see Emmy Wellesz, *The Vienna Genesis* (London: Faber and Faber, 1960), plates 6, 7, and 8; and Kurt Weitzmann and Herbert L. Kessler, *The Cotton Genesis: British Library Codex Cotton Otho B.VI* (Princeton: Princeton University Press, 1986), plates 336–66. For bas relief, see Pamela Z. Blum, "The Middle English Romance 'Iacob and Iosep' and the Joseph Cycle of the Salisbury Chapter House," *Gesta* 8 (1969): 18–34.

18. See Rachel Milstein et al., *Stories of the Prophets: Illustrated Manuscripts of Qisas al-Anbiya* (Costa Mesa, CA: Mazda, 1999), especially 124–30 for the Joseph story. For one artist's illustration of Jami's story, Michael A. Barry, *Figurative Art in Medieval Islam and the Riddle of Bihzad of Herat (1465–1535)* (New York: Rizzoli, 2004), 202.

19. For Ibn Battuta, Ross E. Dunn, *The Adventures of Ibn Battuta* (Berkeley: University of California Press, 1986). For his Anatolian journey, see pages 137–58. A scholarly annotated translation is Hamilton A. R. Gibb, *Travels of Ibn Battuta, A.D. 1325–1354*, vol. 2 (Cambridge, U.K.: Cambridge University Press, 1962), 413–68.

20. See Grace Martin Smith, *The Poetry of Yunus Emre, A Turkish Sufi Poet* (Berkeley: University of California Press, 1993).

21. For this poem, see Arthur S. Napier, *Iacob and Iosep* (Oxford: Clarendon Press, 1916).

22. "The most beautiful of stories" are the words of the Qur'an (xii, 3) describing its own narrative. Here Hamza puts them into Turkish.

23. The first four caliphs were Abu Bakr, Umar, Uthman, and Ali.

24. According to some traditions, Jacob had a number of wives and concubines, each of whom bore him two sons. For the significance of this for Hamza's story, see the translation, ll. 1024 and 1131.

25. The archangel Gabriel (Turkish, *Cibril*) is the conveyor of God's prophetic messages to Muhammad and messenger for and transmitter of God's commands to others as well.

26. Hewing closely here to the Qur'an's elliptical narrative, and aware of possible confusion resulting from it, Hamza alerts listeners to his expansion of the story and explication of information he deemed of interest to his audience. The Qur'anic text has no explanation of who dug the well.

27. For more on Seth and Hud, see Noegel and Wheeler, *Historical Dictionary of Prophets*, 399–400 and 140–42, respectively.

28. For a brief discussion of the merchant's dream and a possible source for some of its imagery, see my "Notes on a Fourteenth-Century Anatolian Turkish Poem," in *Puzzles of Language: Essays in Honour of Karl Zimmer* (Wiesbaden: Harrassowitz, 2011), 230 and 233.

29. Hamza describes Taymus as "Lord of the West" using the Arabic word (*maghreb*) denoting North Africa west of Egypt.

30. Numerous motifs from the Joseph story were referenced or elaborated upon by Muslim sufi poets, foremost among them Farid al-din 'Attar (d. ca. 1200). For Zeliha's withering sigh and several others, see the analytical index ("Joseph") in Hellmut Ritter, *The Ocean of the Soul*, translated by John O'Kane (Boston: Brill, 2003).

31. The mirror, a post-Qur'anic addition to the story, and its symbolism were taken up by Muslim mystics. For a version by Attar, "Story of Joseph and His Looking in the Mirror," see Farid al-Din Attar, *The Ilahi-nama or Book of God* (Manchester: Manchester University Press, 1976), 327–28. That story's sophistication and mystical bent would likely have been lost on Hamza's presumed audience.

32. Hamza's poem ignores the philosophical argument over free will (Joseph's pride) versus predestination (his travails come from God).

33. For more on the formal aspects of Hamza's poem, see my "From Oral Story to Literary Text: Rethinking an Old Ottoman Poem," *Türk Dilleri Araştırmaları* 17 (2007): 177–89. The phrasing of his lines suggests that indigenous rhythms and accentual stress played a key role in their structure and may have been more important than the alien prosody (*aruz*) that the Turks adapted from earlier Persian and Arab poets.

34. For examples of these different sorts of narrator intrusions, see ll. 0068, 0017, 0201, 0187, 0817, and 0912. These frequent interjections, which today's reader may find repetitive and annoying, often help Hamza keep his couplets to the fixed meter of alternating long and short syllables that it is assumed he adopted for his poem.

35. So Jacob's parting words to Joseph—"You, too, leave this city behind" (l. 1452)—may be read as Hamza telling his own audience to prepare for death. For another instance, see l. 0541 and n. 29 thereto.

36. At lines 0512, 0760, 0844, 0930, and 1416.

37. The vivid imagery of these moralistic digressions, especially in that of the longest (ll. 0760–818), likely came into the realm of popular lore from older written accounts. For the translation of one such account (by Abu Layth al-Samarkandi) with close parallels to Hamza's "moral," see Arthur Jeffrey, *A Reader on Islam* ('S-Gravenhage, Mouton, 1962), 236–39. For another account: W. M. Thackston, "The Paris Mi'rajnama," *Journal of Turkish Studies* 18 (1994): 263–85. For illustrations accompanying the preceding source: Marie-Rose Seguy, *The Miraculous Journey of Mahomet: Miraj Nameh*, translated by R. Pevear (New York: G. Braziller, 1977).

38. For a nearly contemporary example of such bardic storytelling, see Geoffrey Lewis, trans., *The Book of Dede Korkut* (Harmondsworth: Penguin, 1974). See also the afterword.

39. A near contemporary of Hamza with the pen name "Yusuf the Meddah" composed a verse romance that bears some stylistic resemblance to Hamza's "Story of Joseph." Yusuf's narrator does not intrude nearly as much, however, into the narrative as does Hamza's. See Grace Martin Smith, *Yusuf-i Meddah, Varqa ve Gulsah* (Leiden: Brill, 1976). For more on

the meddah tradition at a later time, see the now outdated but still useful books by Nicholas N. Martinovitch, *The Turkish Theatre* (1933; New York: Blom, 1968), 21–29, and Metin And, *A History of Theatre and Popular Entertainment in Turkey* (Ankara: Forum, 1963), 28–31. Cf. P. N. Boratav's scholarly overview "Maddah" in *EI2*, v, 951–53.

40. The unique manuscript copy is dated 1545 (932 of the Muslim calendar). For examples of scribal intervention, consider the following. Between the end of the third "moral" (l. 0849) and the resumption of the story, a transitional line (which Hamza elsewhere typically supplies) appears to have been left out. And at line 1094, Joseph's son Mishelum appears to answer a question from Benjamin before it has been asked. (Here the slip may be complicated by Hamza's use of an unusual phrase, presumably derived from oral narrative tradition. For more on this point, see my "From Oral Story," especially 179–85.) Lines 0936–43 repeat quite closely what Hamza has already told us, between 0923 and 935, and I have deleted them in my translation.

41. For more on these, see, respectively, *EQ* iv, 261–63 ("Preserved Tablet"); *EQ* iv, 12–20 ("Paradise"); *EI2* iv, 292–3 ("Izra'il"); and *EQ* ii, 414–20 ("Hell and Hellfire").

42. According to some sources, the well into which Joseph was cast was dug by Shem, one of Noah's sons. And Shem is sometimes confused with Seth, adding to the constellation of details surrounding the figure of this ancient prophet in the Joseph story. See Noegel and Wheeler, *Historical Dictionary of Prophets*, 301.

43. The source of this motif is unknown to me. Receiving something orally seems to be a well-established way of acquiring powers of dream interpretation. See John C. Lamoreaux, *The Early Muslim Tradition of Dream Interpretation* (Albany: State University of New York Press, 2002), 22–23.

44. For a different view of the fairy (*peri*) in Turkish folk belief, see Lewis, *The Book of Dede Korkut*, 140 and n. 96.

45. Qutayfar's disappearance through death is an established feature of Muslim narratives of the Joseph story, not a slipshod mistake by Hamza. The Egyptian ruler, oddly, has the same name ("Al-Rayyan") as that of the bull of early creation stories. See *Kisa'i*, 10.

46. Hamza's reference to "Caesar" (*Qaysar*), anachronistic to our ears, would have been understood as the Byzantine emperor in Constantinople (not any emperor in Rome), although the province in Asia Minor that he ruled was called "Rum" by the Arabs (l. 618). For examples of time warp from the world of European art—of turbaned Ottomans or Mamluks peopling early Christian scenes from Egypt and the Holy Land—see the Metropolitan Museum of Art Catalogue, *Venice and the Islamic World 828–1797* (New Haven: Yale University Press, 2007) and especially the essay by Catarina Schmidt Arcangeli, "'Orientalist' Painting in Venice, Fifteenth–Seventeenth Centuries," 120–39.

47. Joseph's "raining destruction" upon the people of Egypt (l. 1477) was in accordance with Islamic law whereby war could be made upon a community of Christians only if they had refused a call to embrace Islam. If such a community resisted and was conquered, Christian places of worship were often converted into mosques.

48. See Johns, "Joseph in the Qur'an," 30 and 32, respectively (emphasis added).

49. John D. Yohannan has taken "the story of the chaste youth and the lustful stepmother" as the common theme for his anthology: *Joseph and Potiphar's Wife in World Literature* (New York: New Directions, 1968).

50. For instances of each of these in the Turkish text, see ll. 0081, 0147, and 0173.

51. These are Osman Yıldız, ed., *Şeyyad Hamza: Yusuf u Zeliha* (Ankara: Akçağ, 2008); and Ümit Özgür Demirci and Şenol Korkmaz, eds., *Şeyyad Hamza: Yusuf u Zeliha* (İstanbul: Kaknüs, 2008). The latter book, besides giving a modern transcription of Hamza's poem, includes a useful translation into contemporary Turkish and facing facsimile pages of the sixteenth-century manuscript on which their translation (and mine) is based. See my "Reflections on Şeyyad Hamza's Story of Joseph: Apropos Two Recent Publications," *Journal of Turkish Literature* [Ankara] 9 (2012): 9–29.

Translation of the Poem

The Story of Joseph (Peace upon him)
This is "the most beautiful of stories"

Let us begin by recalling the name of God so that His[1] mercy will rain 0001
upon us. "In the name of God"—at the beginning and at the end,
because the sweetness of speech comes through mention of Him. One
of His names is the Merciful. He forgives his slaves. He is also the Par-
doner. He is the Compassionate. He shows mercy toward that slave
who follows His commands. He sees constantly—whatever sin we 0005
commit, and whether even once we express remorse. He is the Com-
passionate. He will pardon us all. He is the Merciful. He will not
show His Hell to the remorseful. He is the Generous. He will count
your sins. He will inform you of them, He will forgive all. He is
generous, He will give you a lofty palace. He is the Merciful. He
will give you houris, each one of them a beauty like the moon.[2]
Give thanks to God, night and day! We commit sins; He excuses
them all.

Now let us invoke blessings on Muhammad, that most laud- 0010
able one, the hope of sinners. If we invoke blessings on him, our sins
will fall away, however many they may be. Blessings from us too on
the friends, those illuminators of the faith, the imams.

Now understand my telling of this tale. I will relate the story of Joseph—how it all happened. I worked day and night to put these
0015 *words into verse. See what a fine story this is. The beauty of its words will wipe away all the cares from any listener's heart. Of all the writings in the pages of the Qur'an, this story of Joseph is the most beautiful. Now listen! Hear what I have to say! I will tell you a story, sweeter than sweet.*

✷

There was a wealthy man in Canaan, Jacob. He was a Prophet. He had a son named Joseph. *Now pay attention to my story, if you have a heart.*

0020 The Prophet Joseph was seven years old, a beautiful boy, like no other. Joseph had a dream one night. The next morning he asked his father, Jacob, about it.

Joseph. Father, I had a strange dream last night. I'll tell you what I saw. Listen, then tell me what it means. I saw the moon and the sun and eleven stars. They all bowed down before me.

0025 Jacob. Son, keep this dream to yourself! Do not tell another soul, let no one hear your dream lest they be angry with you. Your dream is good; you will live in royal splendor. God will make you ruler over all. Your eleven brothers will come to worship you.

0030 Jacob's stepdaughter overheard Joseph recounting his dream. She overheard Jacob's interpretation of it. She went to Joseph's brothers and told them everything she had heard—what Joseph had dreamt and how their father had interpreted it. Joseph's brothers were astonished and confused at what they heard.

JOSEPH'S BROTHERS. If Joseph becomes ruler, he will order us all around. We shall have to submit to his rule. What a disgrace for us!

We will have to wait like servants at his door. Let's bring 0035
him here. We can question him about his dream. He must tell it to us in his own words. We should know his thoughts for ourselves, know his frame of mind. Then we can remove this troublemaker from our midst.

Joseph's brothers summoned him, brought Joseph before them. They took up places around him.

THE BROTHERS. Joseph, what sort of dream did you have
last night? Tell us about that dream you had. And how did
your aging father interpret your dream? Speak up! Tell us about 0040
all that.

So Joseph's brothers made him tell them his dream. Joseph told them what he had seen. Joseph's brothers put their heads together.

JOSEPH'S BROTHERS. How shall we deal with him? If his dream comes true, what will we do then? We must kill him!

The brothers made their plans to kill Joseph. They would take him away. First they led Joseph into Jacob's presence. They made up a story to trick their father.

JOSEPH'S BROTHERS. Father, we are going out to hunt. We 0045
want Joseph to come with us.

Listen now!

JACOB. I had a dream. I saw eleven lambs. While they were grazing, my lambs scattered. A wolf made off with the youngest among them. I fear I will see my dream come true. I will suffer much because of it. You go off to your games. I still fear that a wolf will devour my Joseph.

The brothers, with one voice. Father, while we are with Joseph, how can the wolf snatch him away? We will go all together. How should a wolf approach him then!

Jacob listened to what they said. He moaned, he rose up. *Listen to what he does next.* Jacob washed Joseph's head; he kissed him, embraced him. He daubed kohl around his eyes, scattered rose water over him. He tied a sash tightly round his waist. Jacob entrusted Joseph to his brothers' care. He spoke sternly to them. *Now listen. What God's might achieves!*

Joseph's brothers took him and went off. *Now invoke blessings. Let me relate what happens next.* As the brothers were going along, they took counsel among themselves. They swore an oath to kill Joseph.

Joseph's brothers. Let us kill him—all of us, all together. Then we will repent. God will pardon our sin. When we return home, we shall weep. We shall say, "Father, a wolf snatched Joseph."

Thus Joseph's brothers plotted as they went on their way. They swore an oath making firm their agreement.

Jacob's stepdaughter, Lady Dinah,[3] was pious, honest, trustworthy. *How shall I put it.* She loved Joseph. She came to Jacob.

Lady Dinah. Where is Joseph?

Jacob. His brothers went off with him. They went to hunt deer. Go after them now. Call Joseph back home to me.

Dinah ran after Joseph and his brothers, calling out to them. She overtook them.

Dinah. Joseph, don't go! Come back!

Joseph. No, by God, I won't turn back. I am going with my brothers.

Joseph's brothers kept on. Dinah turned back. She could only call out after them, weeping. Joseph's brothers kept on walking. They disappeared, beyond a mountain. *Now listen to what they did to Joseph.* Having brought him this far, his brothers knocked Joseph down, knocked him out. Then they
all stepped back. Joseph came to; he opened his eyes. He put 0070
himself at Reuben's mercy, but Reuben hit Joseph in the face. He hit him so hard. *How can I describe it to you?*

Simeon also tried to kill Joseph. He thought by killing him, he would be free to go home.

Joseph turned; he looked about for help, first from one brother, then another. One brother hit him so hard he lost consciousness again. When Joseph came to, he begged for pity from another. But that one only hit him harder than the first.
Joseph understood what they were doing, knew they intended 0075
to kill him. Suddenly Joseph laughed. He laughed like no one had ever laughed before.

JUDAH, TO JOSEPH. Brother, why are you laughing? What's come over you? Speak, fortunate one! Tell me.

JOSEPH. When my father entrusted me to you, what did he say? I imagined I was safe, I felt an inner calm coming here with
you. Should a person with this many brothers have so much 0080
trouble! I thought, "Why would one brother hurt another?" This apprehension went through my mind.

When Judah heard these words, he moaned. He burned with compassion for Joseph.

JUDAH. Joseph, come here. Don't worry. By God, I won't kill you.

When Joseph heard these words he put himself at Judah's mercy.

0085 JOSEPH'S BROTHERS, TO JUDAH. Traitor, where is that oath
you swore! Why have you broken your oath? You'll wish you
had kept it!

JUDAH. This business is no good. A man who kills his
brother is no brother at all. If you kill Joseph, God will see
that you burn in the fire of Hell. You will remain in that pit of
0090 Hell forever. No one will come to your rescue. Brothers, come
to your senses; repent your actions. Otherwise you will suffer
God's wrath.

JOSEPH'S BROTHERS. Leave Joseph to us then; we'll kill him.

JUDAH. Listen to me, you fools. Let's put Joseph down the well. Then you can all go, scot-free. What need is there to kill him?

Joseph's brothers agreed. None countered Judah's coun-
0095 sel. They thought it good advice. They forced Joseph towards
a nearby well. *Now listen to what they did to him.* Simeon came
forward. He struck Joseph in the face.

SIMEON. Take off your coat, give it to us!

JOSEPH. Hard-hearted one! Leave me my coat! I'm going to die. I need a shroud.

Reuben came forward. He took Joseph's hand, then let it go. Joseph turned to Judah. He implored him—to no avail.

JUDAH. Put a rope around Joseph's waist to lower him into the well.

0100 They took all of Joseph's clothing. They put a rope around
his waist and began to let him down. *The well is deep.* They cut
the rope so he would fall.

At that moment, a command came to Gabriel.

The Voice.[4] Gabriel, hurry down to Earth! Do not let Joseph fall! Go, find a place for him in the well. Take him a heavenly robe.

Gabriel came to Earth, caught hold of Joseph. He put a robe around his shoulders.

Now here there is a break in the story. I will describe that well to you, tell you who dug it. Invoke blessings on the prophet! Listen to my words. In those days, among the unbelievers there was a man, Sheddad, the Son of 'Ad. He was the one who had that well dug. Hud was prophet then. *Invoke blessings on him for his reward in the Hereafter.* Hud used to read the Book of Seth, day and night. He would teach the ignorant the Straight Path. In that book, God praised Joseph's beauty. Hud read that book, he fell in love with that description of Joseph's beauty. He longed to look upon Joseph's face. Now Hud raised his hands in prayer to heaven.

Hud. God, I pray that I may see Joseph's face.

At that moment, a voice came from God.

The Voice. Hud, go down into the well. When you are seated at the bottom, submit to God's will, remain there for 1,200 years. Only then will you see Joseph's face. He will come to you there.

Hud went, sat down at the bottom of the well. He carried out God's command. Every day in the well a pomegranate came to him from Heaven. Across from him a fine lamp burned. Hud sat—twelve hundred years altogether. Finally Joseph, *Peace upon him*, appeared before him. When Hud saw Joseph, he rose.

Hud. Joseph, come, do not be afraid. I prayed to my God that I might see you. For a thousand years, I have longed to

0120 see you. I have read about your beauty in a book. All this time, I wished to lay eyes on you. Now I have seen you. Thanks and praise be to Him who has let this come to pass. Joseph, know your travails come from God. Your brothers would not harm you of their own accord. This trouble that has come to you, know it is because of Him. Now prostrate yourself before God.

Hud said these things. He kissed Joseph, embraced him.
0125 Then Hud fell down and his spirit left his body. When Hud died, in that well, a command came from God. It was at that moment that Gabriel appeared before Joseph.

GABRIEL. Joseph, do not be afraid. It is ordained that you will exercise great authority in the world.

Then Gabriel went his way. Joseph remained in the well and his heart was full of doubt.

Now I have come back to my story. Listen to what Joseph's brothers did. They slaughtered a kid goat, smeared its blood on Joseph's coat.

0130 THE BROTHERS. Let's take an oath. When we get home, we'll all weep together. We'll say, "Father, a wolf snatched him. We had scattered to hunt deer."

Now there was a big tree[5] by the side of the road. Jacob had sat down there, thirsty and hungry. As he waited, wondering when Joseph would come, he heard a voice above, saying, "Seventy."

0135 JACOB. I wonder if my boy will return in seventy years, or will it be seventy days?

Now there is another saying[6] according to which the voice said, "Look for him in forty years, then you will be consoled."

Jacob, that disconsolate one, arose; he went home. He was overcome with grief; his tears flowed freely. After Jacob entered his house, he heard a sound outside. It was Joseph's brothers. All of a sudden they clamored at the door.

Joseph's brothers. Father, where is Joseph? We were care- 0140
less; then a wolf got him!

When Jacob heard those words, his eyes filled with tears. Jacob was overcome. He collapsed, lost consciousness. Joseph's brothers beat their breasts. When Jacob came to, he opened his eyes.

Jacob. Where is Joseph? Enough of this nonsense!

The brothers, all together. Father, a wolf snatched 0145
Joseph. If you don't believe us, see how his coat is covered with blood.

Jacob. Give me the coat! Let me see it. I must control myself.

Jacob's sons gave him Joseph's coat. The old man held it with his hands. He examined it inside and out. He saw the coat was whole; there was no tear. He was beside himself. Jacob was exhausted.

Jacob. You went off, let Joseph out of your sight. Show me
the mark of the wolf on this coat. Go. Find the wolf and bring 0150
him to me! I will ask him myself whether he killed Joseph. Now bring me the wolf. Otherwise, God's curse on all of you.

Joseph's brothers went off. They caught a wolf. They smeared blood about its mouth, then bound its neck and brought the wolf to Jacob.

Joseph's brothers. Father, this is the wolf that devoured Joseph.

0155 JACOB, TO THE WOLF. Where is Joseph? Tell me. Did you kill my boy? Did you devour him?

God now gave that wolf the power of speech. The wolf spoke. It greeted Jacob, bowed down before him.

THE WOLF. Jacob, come to your senses! You are a prophet.
Prophets do not make false accusations. Give me leave to go.
Wherever I find a wolf I will bring them all here. I did not
kill Joseph, nor did any other wolf. I do not know where your
0160 boy is. If you wish, I will swear an oath that I did not kill
him. I speak the truth to you. I have not told a lie. I have
become separated from my own family. I too suffer the pain
of their loss, day and night. I am beside myself. Believe me.
Let me go!

So Jacob freed the wolf. It went its way. Jacob fell into despair with his longing for Joseph. Day and night, Jacob was consumed by the pain of his loss. His tears flowed freely.

0165 *Now listen, there is more.* In Egypt there was a merchant. One night he had a dream. He found an interpreter who could tell him the meaning of it.

THE MERCHANT. I see myself in Canaan, in the Well of ‘Ad. Before my eyes, the sun sinks down into the earth. The heavens rain pearls. Light spreads everywhere over the earth. Suddenly the sun rises again, up out of my collar.[7] I gather the pearls. That is what I saw in my dream.

0170 THE INTERPRETER. Your dream is auspicious. Give me two gold pieces, I will interpret it for you.

The merchant gave him what he asked, and the interpreter interpreted his dream. He explained the “sun” of the merchant’s dream.

THE INTERPRETER. What you saw there, the place with the sun going down over you—that is clear. Pearls rained down. You collected them. In that place, God will grant you your desire. You will purchase a slave there, and cheaply. He will be handsome. You will covet him.

When you come to sell that slave, his worth will be greater 0175
than all the wealth of Egypt combined. This dream of yours is auspicious. Prepare yourself now and go there. This business augers great good fortune.

The merchant rose and made preparations. He set out for Canaan with his caravan. *To make a long story short*, after the merchant and his men reached their destination, they rested for an hour. Then the merchant ordered that food be brought.

THE MERCHANT, TO HIS SLAVES. Busy yourselves, all of 0180
you. Get up! Go and find the promise of my dream's desire.

The merchant's slaves rose; they did as their master ordered. They looked about, looked everywhere. The merchant himself walked around the well. At this moment, a voice spoke to the merchant.

THE VOICE. Be patient! Come back in fifty years and look again. Then you will find what you are looking for.

The merchant heard these words and set off once more.
After fifty years had passed, he came back to that spot. The 0185
merchant drew his caravan together around the well. This time he commanded his slaves to bring him water. Two slaves hastened to the well. One was named Beshir,[8] the other Mamil. *Remember them!* Beshir lowered a rope into the well. Mamil filled the bucket full of water.

At that moment, Gabriel came and greeted Joseph in the well.

0190 Gabriel. Joseph, know this! Permission has come from God. Stand up, hold onto this rope. The time has come. Prepare to rise up out of the well, with a litany of praise for the Most Holy on your lips.

See how timely this story comes to us! Now Joseph had looked into the mirror, had seen his own appearance, and was amazed: "How beautifully God created me! If I should be sold as a slave, who could afford me? He who would own me would have to give up all his worldly goods."

These were the words that brought catastrophe on Joseph, that
0195 *soon caused him to be sold for next to nothing. His saying "It is I!"*[9]
brought much harm to Joseph. Let these words suffice as warning to you and me both.

Gabriel. Joseph, know now your worth is great!

At that moment, Joseph grasped the rope with both hands. Beshir and Mamil heaved, they hoisted him up out of the well. When Mamil saw Joseph's face, he turned to Beshir, he called out to him.

Mamil. Beshir, this is a slave, a youth with a face as beautiful as the full moon.

0200 Mamil and Beshir repeated the following words to each other.

Mamil and Beshir. Our master's dream has come true.

You would think it was the moon that arose from the well. He who sees Joseph's face is a rich man indeed.

Beshir and Mamil gave the merchant the good news of Joseph's appearance. When the merchant cast his eyes on Joseph, he was overcome by the boy's beauty. Coming to his senses, he took Joseph by the hand. They took Joseph to the tent.

Now Joseph's brothers had climbed a nearby hill. They saw 0205
a caravan camped by the well and hastened toward it.

JOSEPH'S BROTHERS, TO THE MERCHANT AND HIS MEN. Look, we had a slave. We know he came to you. Don't hide him. Hand him over now or there'll be trouble.

Having concealed Joseph, the merchant's men now brought him out from hiding. They were respectful, were afraid. When Joseph's brothers came face-to-face with him, they spoke to Joseph in their own language.

They frightened the boy. Joseph feared for his life. 0210

JOSEPH'S BROTHERS. Merchant, we'll make you a bargain. We'll sell you this slave. Is there one of you who wants a slave of doubtful character? Someone who will take him off our hands, take him away to another land and sell him?

THE MERCHANT. What's wrong with this fellow? Tell me, then I'll make you a fair offer.

JOSEPH'S BROTHERS. For one, he's a liar. He's a thief,[10] and a
runaway too. Keep your eye on him! We'll sell him to you for 0215
what he's worth—silver, gold, copper coins.

THE MERCHANT. I have no gold or silver—but lots of cloth.

THE BROTHERS. What can we do with cloth? We'll sell you the wretch for a few coins.

THE MERCHANT. I have nineteen coppers.

The merchant thought to himself, "At this price I'm getting a bargain."

JOSEPH'S BROTHERS. Then give us your coins and we'll sell him to you.

So Joseph's brothers sold Joseph for nineteen copper coins. 0220

THE MERCHANT, TO JOSEPH. Are you a slave? Tell me honestly. I'll fit my bargaining to the truth.

JOSEPH. Yes, I am a slave. *What he meant was, "I am a slave of God."*

THE MERCHANT. I'll buy him. Tell me again what's wrong with him? Write out a bill of sale and make this bargain right between us.

The brothers wrote the following words on a piece of paper. "We sold you our slave; you know his character. He's a runaway, a liar, a thief. Be careful! Don't let him near your valuables! But his lineage is good. He is a Hebrew slave. We sold him to you fair and square; now he's yours."

So they wrote out a contract. Each of Joseph's brothers renounced his brotherhood.[11] They gave the merchant the bill of sale.

That was how the merchant bought Joseph, how Joseph became his slave. The merchant prepared to take him and set off. He bound the boy hand and foot so he could not escape. Joseph turned his face to heaven, "Almighty God, I put myself at Your mercy."

Joseph, the Prophet, cried like no one had ever cried before. *Don't ask what Joseph's fate was.* They mounted him on a camel and the merchant and his men set off. Later the caravan passed by the grave of Joseph's mother.[12] When Joseph saw the spot, he got down off the camel. He wept, he threw himself upon the grave. He revealed the pain in his heart.

The merchant's men saw Joseph was gone. They sounded the word, scattered in all directions to look for him. All the while, Joseph lay weeping on his mother's grave. One of the merchant's men, a black slave, an Ethiopian, found him.

The slave. Hey, boy, were you trying to run away?

The slave got Joseph up, beat him about the face. He beat him so badly you'd think he wanted to kill him. He took Joseph and put him back on the camel. Joseph let out a moan. Black clouds rumbled, rain poured from the skies. It hailed, it snowed. The plain was awash with all the water.

The merchant doubled over, he cried out.

The merchant. There must be someone here with something to hide, someone with something on his conscience! Whoever you are, speak up now, out with it! Come to the path of repentance so we can be free of this disaster.

The black slave. Master, that Hebrew slave you bought—I beat him within an inch of his life. Maybe that's the cause of all this heavy weather.

The merchant. What are you waiting for! Have him say a prayer for us, anything to stop this flood so we can be on our way!

The merchant's slave went. He found Joseph, kissed his hand, and begged forgiveness for what he had done. So Joseph interceded. At that moment the black clouds broke, the sun came out. The light of dawn spread over the earth.

The merchant saw these things; he contemplated what had happened. He hurried to untie Joseph's hands and feet, dressed him in fine clothes. The people saw Joseph and were amazed.

The merchant, to his slaves. Know this boy as your master, bow down to him now!

The merchant's people obeyed. They did what he commanded.

The merchant and his caravan moved on. They came to a city. *Listen to what I have to say about its people.* The name of the city was Banyas.[13] It was a city full of infidels; they all worshiped idols. When they saw Joseph's face, they were astounded.

People of Banyas. Who created a beauty like you?

Joseph. I know One God. He is the Creator of everything on Earth. He is the All Powerful. He creates what He will. He created the demons. He created the good spirits and the bad. He created mankind. Come! Give up your idols. Accept God, put your faith in Him. Worship and serve Him; confirm His Oneness.

The people of Banyas did as Joseph implored. They professed belief in One God, became pure in faith. They accepted Joseph as their prophet.

Not far from Banyas was another city. Its people, too, were infidels. When those people saw Joseph, they carved an idol that resembled him. The name of that city was Nablus.[14] Its people were fierce, implacable. *Now listen to what I have to say.* Those people could not believe their eyes. They worshipped Joseph, called him "god."

Further along, the caravan came to yet another city, named Jerusalem.[15] Its king too worshipped idols. Day and night he kissed his idols, called them "god." The king had a dream in which Joseph spoke to him. "Come before me, hurry!"

When the king awoke, he got up, mounted his horse, and went out to meet Joseph. The king saw Joseph's face. He was so dazzled by his beauty he forgot who he was. When he came to his senses, the king asked, "Is this man the leader of the caravan?"

The merchant's people. He is the leader of the caravan. His lineage is good. He is a noble man.

The king bowed deeply, took Joseph's hand. Together they proceeded toward Jerusalem. *Now listen to the wonders that Joseph accomplished there.* The king received Joseph as his guest. He gave him a proper reception, put him up. All who saw him were amazed.

The king. Now I'll take you to see my idols.

Joseph. Oh king, listen to me. What sort of idols do you worship?

The king. Come. Together we'll go before them. They will speak for themselves. Let us see what the idols have to tell us.

Joseph. Let us go to your idols, then. You will see what I do to them.

As soon as Joseph set foot in the temple, the king's idols fell to the ground, face down. "God is One. Joseph is His Prophet. Every living thing is His slave." So saying, the idols fell to the ground. They shattered, broke into pieces. The king could not believe his eyes.

The king. I take refuge in the One who created you.

Taking an axe, the king shattered the remaining idols. He untied his sash, put it around Joseph. The king pronounced his belief in One God, professed his faith. He expressed total submission.

Joseph traveled on from there; he reached the city of Arish.[16] *See what he does there.*

When the people of Arish came out to greet him, Joseph became filled with pride. He thought to himself, "God created none more handsome than me. How excellent He created me! Whoever lays eyes on me would die of his desire."

None of the people of Arish wanted to look at Joseph in such a state. *Imagine how miserable Joseph must have felt then!*

Joseph grew sad; his heart was troubled. He heard a voice from above.

The Voice. Joseph! Understand what has happened to you. Dismount! Prostrate yourself now before God.

Joseph dismounted, humbled himself before God, begged forgiveness. Tears poured from his eyes.

Joseph. Almighty God, I turn to You. I beg forgiveness. Pardon my sins.

Weeping, Joseph arose from his prayers. *Whoever saw him in that condition would hardly have believed his eyes.*

Joseph traveled on. *To make a long story short*, finally he reached Egypt.[17] Throughout the land, the people heard of Joseph's arrival. They went out to greet him. Those who saw his face were astonished. They could not believe their eyes.

The merchant put Joseph up in a palace, all roofs and chimneys, full of men and women. The people of Egypt clamored to see him.

The people. Show us the face of that Hebrew slave. We'll give you a piece of gold to look at him.

He who could pay got a glimpse of Joseph. He who could not lived to regret it. Those who saw him were overcome. Some looked and moaned. Some fainted; others lost their wits. Some would have given their lives just to see him.

The next day more came; they paid two gold pieces for a single glance at Joseph's face. The third day, the merchant charged three gold pieces. That was his price of admission. On the fourth day, a man who saw Joseph for five gold pieces thought himself lucky. It went like that for ten days. *Listen to what the merchant does next.*

The merchant took Joseph to the Nile, had him go in the water to bathe. When Joseph wished to wash himself, a fish appeared. It served as a shield, acted as a screen for Joseph. *Some say Joseph stood on the fish.* At that moment, through the grace of God, the fish gained the power of speech.

THE FISH. Joseph, Prophet of God, believe me! How long have I implored God to let me see you. Now through His grace and generosity He has turned the sight of you into my daily bread. I have but one request. I have no young ones. On my behalf, beseech God. He is generous. He will grant your wish.

Joseph prayed; his prayers were accepted. God gave that fish two sons. One was the fish that swallowed Jonah.[18] The other swallowed the ring of Solomon.[19] Thus each received a gift from God. So it was foretold on the Eternal Tablet.

Joseph finished bathing, got out of the river, and left. *Listen now to what the merchant does.* The merchant clothed Joseph in garments that dazzled the eye. *Now listen to what I have to tell you.*

Zeliha was the daughter of the Lord of the West. His name was Taymus. He had an army of more than a hundred warriors. How much that god of the world had given him! He worshipped the cross. That Christian wasted his life for nothing at all.

One night in a dream, Zeliha, daughter of Taymus, saw the image of a man. That image was Joseph's. At a single glance, Zeliha was infatuated with him. *Once afflicted, how can such a person sleep?* Her complexion grew sallow with crying. Her father asked her what the matter was.

Zeliha. In my dream, I saw the image of a man. When I saw that image, I was overcome with love. But I don't know where he is. Better you put me to death or torture me by fire than I remain like this. That's what has happened to me, father.

Ṭaymus. Find out where he is; I will send you to him. Your spirits will revive.

When the new year arrived, Zeliha had another dream. She saw that image again; it spoke to her.

The image. It is I. Open your eyes. Do not give yourself to anyone else.

In her dream, Zeliha rejoiced. But when she awoke, she still did not know where to find that man. The fire of Zeliha's passion only increased. Her agony became unbearable.

Ṭaymus. Zeliha has gone mad. Tie her hands. Her words are senseless. She has lost her mind.

Zeliha. No! I am sane, it is you who is mad, witless one. She who is intoxicated with love can never be insane.

Again the next year, Zeliha saw the same image.

Zeliha. Where are you?

The image. It is I. I am that mighty one[20] of Egypt. Come to Egypt! Find me, see who I am.

Zeliha awoke from her sleep. Her face was radiant. She was free of doubt.

Zeliha. Father, I had that dream again last night. It is good.

The man in my dream said, "Come, seek me out in Egypt. Otherwise stay where you are, be unhappy." Now I understand. He is a ruler, a powerful man. I know who he is. He said, "Come to Egypt. Find me there." I am tormented. That country is far away. Without him I shall die of longing. Do something! Write a letter. Send a messenger to Egypt to inform them of all this.

Let me tell you now how far Zeliha's country was from Egypt. Don't forget to invoke blessings on the Prophet. It would take a horseman six months, traveling day and night, to reach that country.

So Taymus wrote a letter. "Oh, Qutayfar, when will this letter reach you? I have a daughter. She never lets you out of her mind. She speaks of no one else but you. If you wish me to give you my daughter, send a messenger here with your request."

Qutayfar read the letter and understood. He rejoiced. Qutayfar wrote his reply. He dispatched a party with his request to send the woman.

When Qutayfar's letter was received and read, *see what happens.* Zeliha arose, made preparations. She set out for Egypt. *To make a long story short,* when Zeliha reached Egypt, she was received in the ruler's palace. She took her place on the throne. Qutayfar came to her.

Zeliha saw him from behind her veil.

Zeliha, to her attendants. Who is this man? Find out!

The attendants. This is your prince. Be quiet. Come to your senses!

Zeliha heard these words and let out a moan. She collapsed. The servants rushed to her side. Qutayfar saw her but turned away. When Zeliha regained her composure, she got to her feet.

Zeliha. This is not my prince, not the one I saw three times in my dreams.

0365 HER ATTENDANTS. Be patient; you will be united with him. She who is patient knows good fortune in the end.

I have one more thing to tell you, something strange. Whenever Qutayfar asked for Zeliha to sleep with him, a female spirit would come and lie down in her place.

In no time at all, the merchant brought Joseph to the marketplace.

The city criers cried out, "Who will buy this priceless slave
0370 whose face is like the moon? Come, all who would see the
beautiful boy, who would buy the priceless Hebrew slave."

The people came, rich and poor, they gathered round Joseph. They were astonished to see his face, as radiant as the moon.

Zeliha cried out when she saw Joseph from her kiosk. She was overcome by her desire for him.

0375 ZELIHA. This is the one I saw three times in my dreams! Yes! I must collect myself. Whatever money I have, spend it on him. Buy that slave for me, bring him here!

To make a long story short, they told Qutayfar of Zeliha's wishes. The moment Qutayfar laid eyes on Joseph, he was determined to have him.

0380 QUTAYFAR. Merchant, tell me your price. How much do you want for the boy?

MERCHANT. I'll put him on the scales and set his price accordingly.

Qutayfar agreed. They put 5,000 gold pieces on one pan
and Joseph on the other. Joseph went down, the gold went up.
In the end, how shall I say, all the money Qutayfar had in his
0385 treasury was just counterweight to Joseph. Qutayfar grew weak
in the knees.

Qutayfar. I have nothing left in my treasury. Count it out yourself. You've taken all I have. Consider that fair payment for your slave. Show me some respect at least.

The merchant. I acknowledge your payment, I release you from further obligation. I now hand this slave over to you. Know that I have acted in good faith. May our bargain prove auspicious for you.

As soon as he had sold Joseph, the merchant burned with remorse. *Listen to the thought that went through his mind.* "All the treasure in the world was not enough for that boy!"

The merchant, to Joseph. Tell me, who are you? Tell me your name so I know you for sure.

Joseph. Listen. I will tell you who I am, but on one condition—that you tell no one else.

The merchant swore an oath. "I will not tell a soul, I will never tell anyone who you are."

Joseph. I am the son of the Prophet Jacob. My grandfather was Isaac. I am from the family of Abraham.

When the merchant heard those words, he let out a moan. He wept, he grieved.

The merchant. Why didn't you tell me! I would have sent you home immediately to your father and mother. Who are the ones who sold you? What is their relation to you?

Joseph. That's none of my business. I don't tell tales. I stay away from people like that.

The merchant. Then you are from a line of prophets. You are a righteous man.[21] Your prayers are answered. Pray for me now that God may give me a son. That is my only request.

With that, Joseph prayed and his prayers were answered. God gave the merchant forty sons.

Now hear how Qutayfar suffers on account of his purchase, now that his treasury lies empty, and how he regrets that he ever bought Joseph.

QUTAYFAR, TO HIS TREASURER. Go and see if anything is left in my treasury.

0405 The treasurer did as he was told; he went to the treasury. He could not believe his eyes. The treasury was full again. He hastened back with the good news.

THE TREASURER. Your treasury is full to overflowing.

THE SULTAN.[22] Strange! How did that happen?

JOSEPH. God has the power. He is the Almighty. Whatever He wishes He does. Whatever His slaves do, He knows.

THE TREASURER, TO QUTAYFAR. I saw it with my own
eyes. A bird came down from the sky. It alighted upon your
0410 slave. It spoke with the speech of men. "Joseph, prostrate your-
self before God. Know what your true worth is. You looked into the mirror, you were filled with pride at the price you brought. In truth you were sold for nineteen worthless coins. It is true, you suffered, you were mistreated. You saw yourself humiliated. There is no doubt it was that Awesome One who put weight in the balance on your side. Qutayfar emptied his treasury. God made it full again. For your sake He has performed miracles."

0415 QUTAYFAR. Strange! What sort of person is this? While the treasury lies empty, it suddenly fills up again. A bird comes down from the sky and speaks to this slave.

Qutayfar took Joseph; they went to Zeliha. *Now listen to what Qutayfar says to Zeliha.*

QUTAYFAR. The face of this slave is good fortune for us. Let this boy be our son. Treat him with respect. He is a slave but priceless. Show him more respect even than you do me.

Zeliha arose. She embraced Joseph, kissed him. She had 0420
garments cut out for him, a different one for each day. She had precious stones attached to each, stones worth 1,000 pieces of gold!

JOSEPH, TO ZELIHA. Is it right that a slave wear clothes like these?

ZELIHA. There's nothing wrong with a slave like you wear- 0425
ing such clothes.

Zeliha's love of Joseph was beyond comprehension. Wherever she went, she asked, "Where is Joseph?" She forgot everything else but him. Whatever Zeliha saw, she exclaimed, "Ah, this is Joseph." She talked incessantly of him. Wherever she went, she repeated Joseph's name, like a chant.

One day Zeliha took Joseph's hand.

ZELIHA. Come, I will show you my house of idols. You may 0430
see for yourself the faces of those idols. When they see you they will speak.

JOSEPH. Let us go, then, to your house of the idols; let us see what they have to say.

Those two went to Zeliha's house of idols. They went inside, into the presence of the idols.

ZELIHA. Idols, listen! Hear what I have to say! I have fallen in love with this slave. I burn with desire for him. There, I have told you. Now give me strength. Tell me, is it right that I should love this slave?

Now see what God is capable of. God gave the idols the 0435
power of speech. One of them spoke.

THE IDOL. The man you love is a prophet. Thus will he be acknowledged. Come to your senses.

With that, the idol fell to the ground; it broke into bits. All the other idols crumbled and fell into pieces. The shards littered the ground.

ZELIHA, TO JOSEPH. What have you done to my idols? Tell me how this happened!

0440 JOSEPH. My God destroyed these idols. He broke them into bits and scattered their pieces.

ZELIHA. Where is your god?

JOSEPH. He is wherever you look for Him. My God is the All Present. Whatever He wishes He is able to do. He is the All Knowing. He reveals what is concealed. He gives sustenance to all.

ZELIHA. Tell your god these idols must be restored, must be made whole again.

0445 Joseph's lips moved, he spoke. God restored the idols, He made them whole again.

Zeliha saw that; she loved Joseph all the more. That only made Joseph's situation even worse.

When day broke, Zeliha grew pale. Her love of Joseph burned like a fire, it made her ill. One day Qutayfar came and saw Zeliha. He sent for the doctor. The doctor understood Zeliha suffered from the ravages of love; he knew her heart's condition.

0450 THE DOCTOR. Zeliha's pain is extreme because of her love, but she cannot recognize it herself.

ZELIHA. Yet you understand this incurable pain in my heart!

The doctor went away, and Zeliha's nurse came to see Zeliha in his place.

THE NURSE. Poor thing, look at me. What has happened to you? Let me see your face; you're so pale.

ZELIHA. Where is that Hebrew slave? Have you seen him? He did this to me. He left me distraught. If only I had died when I first saw his face.

THE NURSE. That's the way love is. Even if the lover's passion cools, disgrace remains. The fire of love can only sicken a healthy body. He who has not experienced love has no idea of its force! And she who is in love has no mind for good advice. Her eyes are veiled. She cannot see. If only you had told me earlier, I could have found some medicine for you.

ZELIHA. It's not too late. Do what you can! I am consumed by love.

THE NURSE. Have the master builders come; have them make a grand palace for you. They should erect forty columns. They must be of marble. Have them set trees of gold within, with branches of silver. For those trees, they should fashion fruits made of gold. Birds of silver should be set all around. Let them make leaves of green beryl. Have them create the earth of musk and ambergris. Some of the columns should be of glass and some of turquoise, some of ivory. Some too they should make of agate, bright red, and some of chrysolite, green in color. Gold vines should adorn every column. Make the grapes of mother-of-pearl. They must make the throne of gold, very high, with birds of silver off to the side—their heads of beryl and carnelian, their feet of rubies. Fill them with rich scents. Have them spread red satin on the floor, while you sit on the throne, your face like the moon. Have the artists inscribe an image of Joseph on the wall and yours as well. Then summon him to the palace, have him come. Let him see that image of you painted on the palace wall. Let his eyes feast on those figures. Then watch his patience flee as he becomes your lover.

Zeliha found the nurse's advice to her liking; she did not counter with her own reply. While the nurse went about her business, Zeliha fell into despair.

Zeliha, to Qutayfar. Gather together the master builders. Have them build me a sumptuous palace, have them do as I command.

Zeliha drew a picture of herself on the wall of the palace, made her eyes half closed, put kohl around them.[23] Then she summoned Joseph to the palace. Zeliha arose when Joseph entered. She had the gate of the palace closed, she made sure it was secure. When Joseph saw Zeliha, he was overcome, he wept.

Joseph, addressing God. Creator of the Tablet and the Pen, You are Master over all; I am your lowly slave. Mend my broken heart. I take refuge in You now. Watch over me!

When Joseph looked at the wall of the palace, he saw two figures come together, embracing each other as if they were one. They were so vivid you would have thought they were alive.

Joseph, to Zeliha. You have gone to great pains over this palace. How pleasing you have made it. But where is Qutayfar in all this?

Zeliha. Let Qutayfar fend for himself! It is you I am in love with.

What do I care for him! Forget about Qutayfar. Come to me! But mind what you do! Don't leave me again! Come, be here with me.

So Zeliha flattered Joseph. Then she approached him, she leaned over him. With her words, Zeliha slighted neither the artist's craft nor Joseph's beauty. She heaped praise first on Joseph's eye, then on his brow.

Joseph listened to her words and was embarrassed. He thought, "Zeliha has no shame!"

Zeliha. Joseph, listen to me. I saw you everywhere—in our house, in my dreams. When I woke up, I couldn't find you. I was desperate. The first year I cried, night and day. The next year you appeared again in a dream. You spoke to me, told me what to do. "Don't go to anyone else," you said. You spoke beautifully. "You are mine; I am yours," you said. When I saw you the third year, you said, "Come to Egypt, you will find me there."

Zeliha continued. I prepared a caravan of treasure, a thousand mules. I journeyed for six months. I wept day and night. I came here but could not find you; I was beside myself with grief. I fell ill with longing. I died a thousand deaths. I have burned with the pain of my separation from you. Now I have found you; you are mine! Yet you feel no passion for me. You dash my hopes. Come, sit with me a while.

Joseph. Mad woman, I am only a boy of nine or ten. Come to your senses, listen to your own words. I was not even born when this story of yours began.

When Zeliha's slaves let Joseph into the palace, they locked all the gates behind him. At that moment the Devil[24] appeared. He looked and was filled with sedition. He addressed Joseph.

The Devil. There is no way out.

Where should Joseph go? Having entered Zeliha's apartment, Joseph knew his fate was sealed.

At that moment, a voice came from the unknown to the Devil, that accursed one, damned in both worlds: "Take no action counter to God's will. Wake up. Chastity."

With those words the Devil was cheated. He wept. Thus did God spare Joseph from evil.

Moral

A pleasing story comes to mind. Tomorrow[25] *God will bring the dead back to life. The Devil, that accursed one, damned in both worlds, will take great pleasure as he drives people forward toward the Bridge. He will say, "The Bridge is so narrow, so high. The darkness is so vast, like night. No one will cross. They will all fall into the Flames. They will all burn in the end." Then a voice will come from God to that accursed one, that damned in both worlds.*

THE VOICE. Devil, you say "they will burn." I say to them, "Do not despair of My mercy."[26] *I will have mercy on my servants so they shall get across that Bridge. They will enter Paradise and drink of its wine.*

At that moment, the Devil will go blind, he will shed tears. God, through His mercy, will feast His slaves.

Now hear how our story continues. Joseph's heart softened toward Zeliha. He became infatuated with her, he went astray. Joseph saw a hand with writing on its palm, "Fear the day when you shall all return to God."[27] When Joseph saw that message on the hand, he sighed, he repented of his desire. Joseph found restraint.

Zeliha watched Joseph. She cried out, appealed to him. Shame left Zeliha. She revealed her desire. Her tears flowed.

ZELIHA. Joseph, you set my soul on fire. Sit with me a 0525
while. What is your desire? Look at me! I am wretched. Make me whole again.

As Zeliha spoke these words, Joseph felt his own desire return. At that moment, a crack opened in the wall of the palace and again a hand appeared. This time the hand spoke to Joseph, "This way! Fear God! Do not give in to your desire! Mortal creature, why do you pursue your evil ways?"

Joseph saw the hand. He came to his senses, held firm 0530
against his desire.

When Joseph resisted his impulse, Zeliha went wild. *See what she does next.*

Zeliha stood up and embraced him then. *What else could she do! She was in love, her soul ablaze.*

Once more Joseph's desire was aroused. Once again the hand appeared. On it was written, "And thou shall not commit adultery."[28] Joseph saw it, again he pulled back.

Time passed. And again Joseph was filled with desire for 0535
Zeliha. *Now see what God accomplished through His power.*

This time the very wall of the palace split open. A figure resembling Jacob appeared. Joseph was dumbfounded.

THE FIGURE. Joseph, repent! Turn away from that sin. Seek forgiveness. Banish this thing from your heart! How can a prophet commit such an act!

Joseph was ashamed in the presence of that figure; he turned away.

ZELIHA. Wait, you! Come back!

Joseph's desire for Zeliha returned once again. The figure 0540
reappeared. *See what it says.* "And whoever does"[29] will receive

his punishment in Hell. *What that means is, He who commits adultery will be consumed in the Fire.*

When he heard those words, Joseph repented again; again he turned away from desire.

Time passed; yet once again Joseph broke his vow. He gazed at Zeliha with lust in his heart.

At that moment, an angel descended from the sky. It took
0545 hold of Joseph from behind. When the angel squeezed him all the lust drained out of Joseph's body, through his fingers.[30] His passion cooled. Joseph became calm.

God opened the gate of chastity for Joseph, and he restrained himself. He retreated from his desire. But Zeliha did not give Joseph a chance to reach the door. She overtook him, grabbed him from behind. Joseph's shirt tore. As those two struggled, Qutayfar appeared at the door.

ZELIHA. Qutayfar, this boy mistreats me. Teach him a
0550 lesson! He has crude intentions toward me. I tell you, scare the wits out of him, throw him in prison! Maybe then he'll reform.

JOSEPH, TO QUTAYFAR. Zeliha lies. She is the guilty one. Let this infant here be my witness. Ask him, in his cradle. Know, in this affair, I am blameless.

ZELIHA. What can a newborn babe say? This infant does not yet know how to speak.

0555 JOSEPH. My God has the power to let this infant speak. He will talk. You will be amazed, you will know my innocence. Ask him. He will say who the guilty party is.

QUTAYFAR, TO THE INFANT. Who is guilty here?

Through the power of God, the infant spoke.

THE INFANT. If Joseph's shirt is torn in front, if the back is 0560
whole, then Zeliha is right, and Joseph lies. That means Joseph slanders Zeliha.

Qutayfar looked, he saw the shirt was torn in back. He knew Zeliha was lying. Qutayfar admonished her, he turned away.

ZELIHA, TO JOSEPH. Come here. Do you see what Qutayfar has done for us? He has left us alone. Pay no more attention to all this talk.

JOSEPH. Don't you see what happened, what that baby said? 0565
God gave him the power of speech, had him give witness to what you did. Have you not yet repented?

ZELIHA. How should I repent? My soul is overwhelmed by love. I'd sooner die! You made me fall in love with you. Good for you! My love for you has made me the scandal of all Egypt.

It was true. Throughout Egypt women everywhere were gossiping about Zeliha.

WOMEN OF EGYPT. Disaster has struck Zeliha. She fell in 0570
love with that Hebrew slave. While the two of them were talking, Qutayfar came upon them. He admonished Zeliha. Then he left. He saw them but he didn't get angry at her! A woman who falls in love with a slave is no doubt mad, but she who throws herself on him is as good as dead.

Now see what became of those women who carried on about Zeliha!

Let this story be a warning for us. She who slanders another 0575
will either apologize or get her just reward. But she who washes her hands of evil will escape censure. Hold your slandering tongue! Otherwise you reap what you sow.

Zeliha heard the gossip. She had the women brought to the palace. All the while she kept Joseph in a separate room. When the women came to the palace, Zeliha ordered that oranges be brought. *That was the custom of the Egyptians. Whoever provided hospitality would first offer oranges to her guests. Then she would serve the meal.* So Zeliha offered each of her guests an orange and a knife.

Zeliha, to the women. Don't cut until I tell you. Then she called out, "Joseph, where are you?"

Joseph appeared, his face radiant as the moon. It lit up the room. When the women saw his face, they became confused, they were overcome.

Zeliha. Now cut your oranges. But mind your knives.

Each of the women picked up her knife, but instead of cutting the orange each cut her own hand. Still they didn't realize they had cut themselves; they didn't feel the pain.

The women. This is no mortal.[31] He is an angel.

Zeliha. Did you see him, the one who torments me day and night? You looked at his face just once and didn't realize you'd cut yourselves.

And you wonder at my obsession! A glimpse of his face and you lost control of yourselves. And you reproach me for falling in love with a slave! Now you know who my love is.

The women. It is right that she fell in love with him, sacrificed herself for him.

The women went about their affairs, still dazed. Zeliha fell deeper into despair over her love for Joseph.

Zeliha. Joseph, listen to me. Or I'll have you thrown in prison. Don't toy with me. Don't give me impossible advice. Look at what has happened to me.

Joseph. No, I won't do what you want. You do what you will!

Zeliha was furious with Joseph. She berated him. She undid his sash, took off his robe.[32] She took Joseph and went to the king, Reyyan.

Zeliha, to Reyyan. May you have a thousand slaves like me! Now throw this wretch of mine in prison. Let him relent! He behaves insolently toward me.

Reyyan. He's your slave. Do what you will with him.

Zeliha had Joseph put in prison. She left him there; that's how she tortured Joseph. Let him rot!

Everyone who comes into this world will leave it in the end. Now see how God dictates the fate of others.

One day Qutayfar, the sultan, fell ill and died. Zeliha was left a widow. Qutayfar's brother, Reyyan, became king in his place. On his accession to the throne, Reyyan freed all the prisoners of the former ruler, except one. Joseph alone remained in prison.

Now Gabriel descended from heaven again. He greeted Joseph.

Gabriel. Joseph, be patient; put up with this punishment a while longer. Everything resolves in time. Soon you will find favor and fortune. You will know happiness, you will wear silk.

Gabriel brought with him a stone from heaven. God had created it, white like a pearl. Gabriel put it in Joseph's mouth as though conveying an edict from God. The stone gave Joseph the power to interpret dreams through understanding them.

Listen, there is yet another story. I will tell it to you.

Caesar, ruler of Rum, one day addressed one of his men.

Caesar. This is my command. Go to Egypt. Take my greetings to the ruler of the people there. Give him my message. The cupbearer should poison Reyyan. The chief steward should collaborate with him.

Caesar's man did as he was told. He went to Egypt; he informed the two men of Caesar's wishes. In the meantime, the king, Reyyan, got wind of the matter. He seized the men, had them put in prison.

These three, the cupbearer, the steward, and Joseph, told each other the crimes of which they stood accused. They revealed their woes, commiserated with each other. They wept together, each lamenting his own fate. One night, both cupbearer and steward had dreams.

Listen to what each of them saw.

In his dream, the cupbearer took three bunches of grapes and squeezed them. He put the juice in a wine cup. He had his master drink the juice. That's the end of the dream.

The steward, in his dream, saw three ovens. He baked three loaves of bread and carried them on his head. While he was taking the bread to his master, a voice came to him: "Stop there." The steward remained as if rooted to the ground. Birds flocked from the sky, settled on the steward's head. They snatched the loaves and flew away. The steward awoke from his dream but could not understand it.

The steward and the cupbearer told their dreams to Joseph. Each related what he had seen.

The steward and the cupbearer, together. Tell us the meaning of our dreams. What do they portend?

Joseph, to the cupbearer. Understand your dream. Things will turn out well for you. Three days from now they will take you out of here. They will bestow a robe of honor on you. You will be comfortable. You will attain prosperity, find happiness and contentment.

Joseph, to the steward. By God, three days from now they will take you away too. They will hang you and leave your body there. Your flesh will stink. Birds will come and eat your brain.

When the steward heard that, he was terrified.

The steward. That wasn't my dream; I lied.

Three days later, they took the steward away, set up a gallows, and hanged him there.

As for the cupbearer, they honored him, gave him a fine robe. They invoked countless blessings upon him. They brought a horse for him to ride. *Now hear what Joseph has to say.*

Joseph. I have interpreted your dream. But only God knows when your life will come to an end. When you go and see the king, remember me well with your words. I have told you my story. You know I am blameless. Now go and tell him that.

So the cupbearer returned to his place at the court, but Joseph remained alone. At that time, Gabriel descended again from heaven.

Gabriel. Joseph, I have come with questions for you. Tell me. Who caused Jacob to love you? Speak! Who saved you from your brothers? Speak! Who spoke to you as a loyal friend? And who removed you from the well? Speak! Who shielded you from that woman, Zeliha? And who protected you from Qutayfar? Who was it who gave speech to that infant? Who was it who did all these things for you? Speak![33]

Joseph. Those things all came from God.

Gabriel. And what did you do? You failed to bring God's name to your lips, even once. Instead you looked to nonbelievers for your salvation.

When Joseph heard Gabriel's words, he prostrated himself before God.

Joseph. All Powerful Lord, I have come to You. I repent of my ways. Forgive my sins.

Joseph wept. He felt remorse, he repented. His repentance was accepted. And again Gabriel came to him.

Gabriel. Joseph, God sends greetings. After one year, He will make you ruler over all Egypt. All the people in Egypt will bow down before you.

When Joseph heard Gabriel's words, he prostrated himself, gave thanks to God.

In Joseph's prison cell there was a terrace. He used to rest there. One day an Arab approached from far off. As Joseph observed him, the Arab came closer. *Listen to what he has to say.*

The Arab. I've come from Canaan. Hear me out. Your father, Jacob, worries endlessly about you. He's blind from weeping. All he can say is "Joseph," night and day.

The Arab sat down in front of Joseph's cell. With a stick he started to beat his camel, forcing it to lie down.

Joseph. Come over here. Don't beat your animal. Speak up! Where are you from? What news do you have?

The Arab. My home is Canaan. I am a merchant, a stranger[34] here, far from home.

Joseph. What have you brought with you? Tell me! May God grant you success in your labors.

The Arab. I bought a load of goods. I've made a profit—an Egyptian gold pound.

Joseph. Did you see a tree back there, where you came from, a very big tree?[35] It should have eleven branches. Another was cut off, better than the others. The tree weeps for that missing branch. Do you understand? Have you seen such a tree?

The Arab. There is such a tree. I have seen it. It weeps every day for the missing branch. Your description fits Jacob. I understand you. It is extraordinary.

Then Joseph realized his father's situation. He buried his head in his hands; he wept openly.

Joseph. When you get back to Canaan, give my greetings to that man. Tell him there is a stranger, in Egypt, someone far from home. Say, "That stranger sends you greetings." Make those your words.

Joseph gave the Arab a bracelet made of red rubies, worth 10,000 pieces of gold.

The Arab took the bracelet; he prepared to set off on his journey. In time he reached Jacob's house.

The Arab. Where is the Prophet Jacob?

Jacob's stepdaughter. Who are you? What do you want? What news do you bring? Speak up!

The Arab. Tell Jacob to come outside. I've just come from Egypt. I bring greetings to him from a stranger there.

The girl went inside, related what the Arab said.

Jacob. Tell him to come in.

The Arab entered; he greeted Jacob.

The Arab. In Egypt there's a wretched soul confined in prison. He suffers much on your account. He sends his

greetings, asks for your prayers. He asked me to remember him to you. “Give him my greetings.
0690 Have him pray for me.” There, I’ve given you his greetings. Now make sure you pray for him.

JACOB. Did you ask his name? Did you find out who he was?

THE ARAB. He spoke well. I didn’t ask his name. His face was covered.[36]

JACOB. Let me give you something for your trouble. Tell me what you need. I’ll give you what I have.

THE ARAB. I have no need for material goods. That stranger
0695 rewarded me well. He gave me a priceless bracelet, worth more than all the gold in Egypt. My only request of you is a prayer from God for this poor soul.

Jacob prayed for the Arab who went his way. He was left to brood over that strange soul.

Jacob wondered to himself, could that wretched one who wishes for a prayer from his prison cell be my Joseph?

JACOB PRAYED. God, whether it is Joseph or not, save that poor soul from that place. Grant him deliverance.

0700 *Now let me tell you the story of Joseph’s circumstances in prison, in Egypt.*

After a whole year had passed Gabriel, *peace upon him*, came again to Joseph. He brought good tidings.

GABRIEL. Joseph, you will be freed soon, but first you must prostrate yourself before God. Henceforth you will have authority to rule as sultan. Now hurry, rise and acknowledge your submission to God.

Joseph arose, performed his ritual ablutions. He prostrated himself before God; he thanked and implored Him.

Listen to the plight of the king, Reyyan; how he had a dream 0705
and how Joseph interpreted it.

In his dream, the king saw seven cows, all of them fat. They grazed peacefully. And the king saw seven more, all lean. Those seven swallowed up the seven fat ones. The king also saw seven stalks of fresh wheat, and seven dry. All together the stalks flew up into the sky and disappeared.

The king's interpreters could not interpret the dream, could not even understand it.

The interpreters. We do not know what to make of this.

King Reyyan grew angry with his interpreters. Some he 0710
banished; some he beat. Just then, as the king lashed out at
them, the wine steward[37] remembered Joseph. He nodded his
head.

The king. Why did you nod your head just now? What were you thinking? Tell me.

The wine steward. There's a boy in prison. He knows about dreams, he's very smart.

The king. How do you know that? Tell me about this boy. 0715

The wine steward. I had a dream myself, in prison. I asked him about it, he interpreted it for me. It turned out just as he said. What he foretold came true. That's why I nodded my head.

The king. Go to that boy then. Tell him my dream. Ask him about it. Come back and tell me what you learn.

The wine steward. I will do as you say, but first I have a
promise to keep. Before I came here, the boy said to me, "When 0720
you see the king again, don't forget about me. I've committed

no crime." He wept as he told me. I did forget. For a whole year, I've given his words no thought at all.

The king. That boy believes in One God. He holds Him responsible for good and evil. Go, give him my greetings. Have a word with him.

The wine steward returned to Joseph. He showed his respect, covered his face with his sleeve. He told Joseph about the king's dream, told him every detail.

Joseph. The seven fat cows the king saw, and the lean ones eating them; the seven stalks of green wheat that disappear into the sky and the seven dry stalks that do the same. There will be seven years of rain. Crops will grow. The land will be productive. Then there will be seven years of scarcity. The rains will not come, nothing will grow. There will be famine. After seven years, the people will be exhausted.

The wine steward listened to Joseph's words. Then he returned to the king. King Reyyan listened to what the steward told him; he was truly astonished.

The king. Go! Bestow a ceremonial robe on that boy, something that will dazzle the people. Treat him with deference and bring him to me.

The wine steward went back to Joseph. He kissed his hand, bestowed on him a ceremonial robe.

The wine steward. Joseph, get up! The king summons you. These are good portents. Come with me!

Joseph. No; I am not going anywhere until the king stops speaking about my "guilt." Have him gather together those women of Egypt! Zeliha should be there too. Then have him seek out my guilt from them. Have them tell him how they cut their hands.

The wine steward informed King Reyyan of Joseph's words. 0740
The king brought the women together into his presence. Zeliha
was among them. *Listen to my story.*

King Reyyan. Tell me, why did you cut your hands? Don't hold anything back. Tell me the truth. Tell me Zeliha's role in this.

Zeliha spoke up, before the rest. She told the story of her pain. She did not flinch.

Zeliha. I am the guilty one. I fell in love with my slave, and 0745
he did not obey me. He did not have any feeling for me. That is
why I locked him up. I loved him. I thought he would change!

When King Reyyan heard Zeliha's words, his blood boiled, his eyes burned with rage. He was furious.

King Reyyan. Take her away! Don't let her say another word.

They took Zeliha away. King Reyyan brooded over Joseph.
He gathered everyone. Together they went to the prison. The 0750
king burned incense along the road. He had a golden throne
set up, had it placed in front of Joseph. When the prisoners saw
those honors for Joseph, they wept for joy.

The prisoners. Joseph, remember us too. Perhaps the king will honor your requests on our behalf.

So Joseph, with pure heart, made petitions on their behalf.
The king, in turn, pardoned them for Joseph's sake. However 0755
many they were, the king set them all free. Then Gabriel came
to Joseph.

Gabriel. Joseph, ascend this throne; earthly rule is now granted to you.

Joseph ascended the throne. The people carried him off to the city. So it was that Joseph became sultan. They all bowed down before him, weak and strong. King Reyyan embraced Joseph as well.

THE KING. You have become ruler over all.

The king scattered symbolic offerings all about.

Moral

Another pleasing story comes to mind here. Offer prayers, and God's humble servant will relate it to you.

At the Day of Reckoning, God, the Illustrious One, will issue His commands. Gabriel will come and stand [on the Bridge] above the Fires of Hell. He will see many mortals burning in that fire, consumed and wailing together. Among them He will see certain creatures with their faces, their flesh, even their hearts, engulfed in flames. Except for their faces, all the other parts of their bodies are burned. Gabriel will see those creatures and be astonished that their faces are untouched by the fire.

GABRIEL. To which community do you belong? Your faces remain fresh and whole. Tell me, why have they not burned?

THOSE CREATURES. We are the ones who have sinned. Day and night we burn in the Hellfire. The fires of Hell are never extinguished; that way God can go on burning us forever. He does not let our faces burn, but all the rest of our bodies, all our limbs, day and night. He has set aside this part of the Fire for our ritual prostrations. He does not let the places around us burn. The awesomeness of this Fire has robbed us of our wits. It has burned us terribly. We have forgotten the name of our prophet. Who is he? Where is that leader of ours?

GABRIEL. Might your prophet's name be Muhammad?

On hearing that name, the lamentation of those creatures only 0775
increases.

Those creatures. *Yes! He is the one who will forgive all our sins. Muhammad is our hope. Tell him of our situation, just as you have seen us. He is our hope. Muhammad must intercede for us so God will pardon our sins.*

At that moment, Gabriel will reach Muhammad. The archangel will relate to him the circumstances of the prophet's own community.

Gabriel. *I visited Hell. I saw people there. One of them said* 0780
to me, "I'm thirsty! Even if it were poison I would drink it." Another said, "I'm hungry. Even if it were oleander[38] *I would eat it." Malik*[39] *arrived; he takes water used for washing the dead and gives it to them to drink. That only increases their burning. Just listen to*
what happens to some of the others. Their brains boiled over, all 0785
rubbing together; their flesh flared up, it smoldered. Each of those creatures wept in that domain of Hell; those that were already burned caught fire all over again and were returned to the flames. Each of them was crushed; they were bent double at the waist. There was a wailing there as they were arrayed in groups. Red hot chains were attached to their waists. They caught fire and burned like coal. When those creatures saw me, they knew who I was.
Through me they have sent greetings to you. They pleaded for pity, 0790
hoped for relief. Messenger of God, come to the aid of your people. Appeal to God on their behalf. Intercede for them; may your prayers be accepted by God.

Listen now to what Muhammad, Beloved of God, does on hearing these words from Gabriel. He will prostrate himself at the foot of God's Throne.

Muhammad. For my sake, forgive my people.

God will say, "I have forgiven those people. Whatever sins they have committed, however bad, I have absolved your people, for your sake. I am the Munificent. I have acted with generosity. Good news now for them, to be saved. Take them and lead them. Let them enter Paradise."

Then Muhammad will come back and speak to his people.

Muhammad. You have been set free.

When Muhammad's people hear these words, when they see his face, they will invoke countless blessings on Muhammad. And the Fire of Hell will recede; it will vanish from the presence of his people.

Muhammad will proceed to raise his people up out of Hell. He will take his place at their head and lead them away. In the Sea of Living Creatures,[40] *he will wash the filth of Hell Fire from them. Muhammad's people will rise up out of that sea. Each one's blackened skin will become pure white. Still, the mark of Hell will be on all their foreheads. They will enter Paradise with that mark. When the people of Paradise see them coming, they will recoil from them.*

The People of Paradise. The rebellious ones have arrived from Hell.

Those refugees from Hell will turn away; they will come back to Muhammad, hope of sinners. They will stand before him wailing, ashamed of this mark.

The refugees from Hell. Free us of this mark or send us back so that we may burn again in the Fire! How shall we enjoy Paradise with this mark? Better that we return to Hell!

When Muhammad—that Chosen One, Sublime, Purified—hears these words, he will erase that mark on each of their

foreheads with his ring. Those marks will vanish. Muhammad's people will rejoice. At that moment, each of them will give thanks. Then Muhammad will feast them all. To each he will give a fine tall palace, to each a moon-faced beauty. He will give them garden
pavilions strewn with carpets and with a tall throne in each. He 0815
will make his face a source of nourishment daily for them all. The believers will see that face and be amazed. On seeing it, the very radiance of those believers will also increase.

Lord, make that face of Muhammad a source of nourishment for us too! Listeners, offer prayers. Let Muhammad, whose name is mentioned in the Qur'an, rejoice as well. He is the intercessor for us all. He will appeal on our behalf on Judgment Day. God will accept his word; He will show mercy on us.

So Joseph now made his requests of King Reyyan, that idol
worshipper, on behalf of all his prison-mates. Reyyan accepted 0820
Joseph's intercession. He freed the prisoners. They went their way.

Since Muhammad is our intercessor, is there any doubt that God will show compassion for you? Now listen to what King Reyyan does.

KING REYYAN, TO JOSEPH. What must we do about my dream?

JOSEPH. We must empty the treasury. Whatever treasure 0825
you have, entrust it to me.

The king counted his wealth, entrusted it all to Joseph.

Joseph ordered the people of Egypt to plant as many crops as possible. When the time was right, they harvested the crops. For seven years, rich and poor alike filled their storerooms to overflowing.

When those seven years passed, the drought began. Joseph
0830 commanded the people not to plant. For seven years, there was no rain and there was no grain. There was only scarcity. There was no breeze.

The people of Egypt traded their gold and silver for grain so they could eat. The next year, they spent the last of their silver. The third year, they brought their animals, horses and mules, and gave them to Joseph in return for grain. The fourth year, the people, both healthy and sick, sold their orchards and
0835 vineyards. That was all they could do. The next year, nothing remained to give to Joseph; they got nothing in return. The sixth year, they sold their sons and daughters to Joseph—that's how they survived. In the seventh year, all the people of Egypt became Joseph's slaves.

With still three months left of the year, the entire supply of grain was gone. Gabriel came to Joseph.

0840 GABRIEL. God commands you: "Leave the city. Once a month the people will see you; they will forget about eating and drinking. When they look upon your face all their needs will be met, body and soul."

So once a month they brought Joseph out for all the people to gaze upon. One glimpse of his matchless face satisfied them all, young and old, healthy and frail.

Moral

Listen! A pleasing story comes to mind. This humble slave of God will relate it to you.

0845 *At the Day of Judgment, when the People of Paradise finally enter heaven, they will view that place in all its glory.*

The People of Paradise. "Oh, Lord, grant us what You promised."[41] *Generous One, bring to fruition what we desire, so we may see Your Face, Compassionate One.*

That is what Muhammad, the Chosen One, meant when he declared, "What that Generous One promises, He fulfills."[42] *When God manifests Himself to them, they will all forget Heaven.*

At that time, the merchant who sold Joseph also came before him. He too became Joseph's slave, together with all his sons. In return he took his share of grain; he was able to eat and gain strength. Now it was Joseph who assumed the role of the master. Once again Gabriel came to Earth.

Gabriel. Know now who is the slave. Prostrate yourself before God! How many were your slaves. Leave this city, Joseph. Whomever you encounter first, make him your chamberlain, take him as your adviser.

When day dawned, Joseph rose. He saddled his steed, he mounted up.

Now Joseph had a splendid horse. Whenever Joseph mounted, that stallion whinnied so loudly. How shall I describe it? The people of Egypt would all know that Joseph had mounted his steed. His troops and retinue would gather at his side. That stallion stood still so Joseph could mount. The stallion whinnied. The people heard. The troops and retinue gathered. What an act! Bravo!

As Joseph rode out of the city, he saw a stranger. The man's clothes were torn. He was frail, a solitary soul. Joseph thought, "What good is this fellow? He's too weak even to open his mouth."

At that moment, Gabriel reappeared.

Gabriel. Joseph, God sends you bountiful greetings. "Let Joseph repent for his haughty words. Let him come to his senses. That stranger he has encountered is his adviser. Let Joseph know!" Joseph, you failed to respect that man. Shame! Show him due regard now with a fine robe. Treat him well!

Joseph did as Gabriel commanded. He dressed that stranger in a handsome robe. He turned his face to God, begged forgiveness.

Now listen to Zeliha's situation. I'll describe her circumstances to you.

Zeliha had become destitute; she was impoverished. Not a coin to her name, not a crust of bread to eat. She wore a blanket, tied round her waist with a rope of grass. She had gone blind with all her weeping. Her only words were, "Joseph, Joseph," day and night. She wept, she moaned, hoping Joseph would hear, take pity on her.

But Joseph was aware of none of this. Even had he seen Zeliha's face, he would not have known her. Whenever she went out, she took the road he traveled, hoping he would pass. She made that road her constant companion. Zeliha could not take her eyes off the road. She had a house built to one side thinking if Joseph passed he would hear her cries. Zeliha engaged a woman to keep her eye on the road.

Zeliha. If Joseph approaches, get me up. I will moan and tear my breast. Maybe then he'll see my sighs and take pity on me—even speak to me.

So it happened one day that Joseph rode past. The woman came and told Zeliha.

The woman. Quick, get up! Your Joseph is near. Get up.

The woman took Zeliha's hand and brought her to the side of the road. Zeliha sat down, crying.

Zeliha. Joseph, have pity on me. Help me! I must have fallen. Give me a hand.

Joseph did not hear Zeliha or her sighs. Heartbroken, Zeliha returned to the house. She was furious; she reproached her idol.

Zeliha. I have worshipped you, day and night. What good did it do me! You left me destitute, hungry, helpless. I took you to be my god, bound myself to you. What did I get! Once I was a lady in Egypt. Joseph started out a slave; see what he's become: a ruler, renowned. His god did that for him!

With that, Zeliha dashed the idol to the ground. It smashed and flew into pieces.

Zeliha. I believe in the One God. I turn to You. I repent. No doubt, You are the All Generous. Now answer my need, work your influence on Joseph that he may return my love.

Another day came. As Joseph passed by, Zeliha stood at the side of the road and began to speak.

Zeliha. Joseph, wait! Listen, look at me. Have pity on me! Do something.

Joseph. Who are you? What do you want?

Zeliha. Don't you recognize me? I am Zeliha, that wretched slave of love. I am the one who bought you. You are my slave. Restore me to my former self. All my wealth went for your sake. I love you with all my heart and soul, day and night.

Joseph. Show me proof of what you say. Show that to me so I may know it clearly.

Zeliha. Give me your whip. You will see, you will be amazed!

Joseph held out his whip to Zeliha. She took it and moaned. The whip smoldered, it fell to the ground in flames.

Joseph saw that and was amazed. God had given her so much love.

So Zeliha and Joseph became engrossed in each other's company. Gabriel returned. He brought greetings from God.

Gabriel, to Joseph. Take Zeliha, make her your companion. Marry her.

Keep God's command. He has the power to transform her. He can make her youthful again, and beautiful. Her sightless eyes will see again.

Joseph turned back. When he reached his palace, Joseph found his heart opened to Zeliha. He seated himself upon his throne. Joseph summoned Zeliha, had her brought to the palace.

At that moment, Gabriel returned. The angel caressed Zeliha. She became fourteen again. Her face was like the full moon. Sight returned to her sightless eyes.

King Reyyan arrived. He paid the dowry to Zeliha.

They feasted. Then the people dispersed. *God has the power to do what He will. See how I have brought the story to this point.*

Joseph and Zeliha entered the bridal chamber. Zeliha became young again. *How miraculously God had preserved her youth.* Joseph was astonished.

Zeliha. My God watched over me. His power saved me for you. He created a female spirit. Whenever Qutayfar desired me, that spirit would come and lie by his side in my place.

So it was that God gave Joseph fourteen sons[43] by Zeliha. *That is the truth.* Mishelum was the eldest, the firstborn. He was smarter than the others. Of the rest one was Shemdin, another Mamil.[44] Qasan was the name of the last.

Here I have summarized the story. Let us invoke blessings upon Muhammad from God. There is still more strange to come. But, again, blessings so our hearts will rejoice.

When Joseph became sultan, when all the people in Egypt acknowledged his rule, he linked all the roads into a network. He ordered that they all be joined together in a single road. He had them all enter the city by a single gate. All the people should come and go through that one gate. Joseph installed a watchman who would question those who entered the city. If those travelers would not reveal their identities, they would be turned away.

Joseph's intention was to see his brothers. If they came, he would recognize them all together. Listen! Once he found them, he had that network demolished.

Moral

Another story has come to me; let me tell you. But first, offer prayers, make them loud.

At the Resurrection, our God commands that all the walls of Paradise be filled in. He will create seven bridges across Hell. Those consigned to Hell will gather together. God will have them questioned. Angels will watch over them and question them about their worldly acts. Some will cross easily; others will fall into the Hellfire.

Those who cross will enter Paradise and feast on grilled meat; those who don't will endure the worst tortures.

[Lines 936–43 omitted][45]

Now listen. See where this story is going.

0945 Word went out far and wide, "Those who want grain, come to Egypt and get it." And the people came, all seeking grain.

In Canaan, Jacob was worn out, his stomach was empty. He summoned his sons; he revealed his plans.

Jacob. I've heard about this man. He's of right religion. What they say is true. He who goes against him must be of little faith. When you get there and make your request, he will treat you respectfully, give you the grain you ask for.

0950 Ten of Jacob's sons were present. They made preparations and set out for Egypt at dawn. One of the brothers remained behind.

To make a long story short, when Joseph's brothers got to Egypt, they were granted permission to enter the city. They saw that the prophet Joseph gave bread to every Arab, wherever he came from. To every one he gave a whole loaf, all day long.

0955 Joseph's brothers observed him; they were astonished at his generosity. Everyone who wanted grain got an entire load, worth two hundred gold pieces. *And when I say a load, I mean a load fit for a camel, not just a sack for a mule.*

Joseph watched from his kiosk. The moment he saw his brothers, Joseph was overcome. When he came to, when he opened his eyes, his vizier spoke up.

0960 The vizier. You fell down, lost consciousness. Collect yourself. What happened?

Joseph. Ask those men how long they've been here. Tell me what you learn.

The vizier. They've been here five days. They're from Canaan; they've come to buy grain.

Joseph. Summon them to the palace, treat them with respect.

The vizier went, had Joseph's brothers brought to the palace. He made them comfortable, fed them and lavished gifts on all of them. While the brothers ate, the vizier went to pray.

THE BROTHERS. That mighty one thinks we have lots of gold. That's why he treats us so well, else he wouldn't have bothered with us.

JUDAH. He has heard of our father. On his account, he behaves as he does.

Joseph overheard his brothers. His heart ached; he could not keep from crying. He concealed his face and came down from his kiosk. He approached his brothers, questioned them.

JOSEPH. Where are you from? How many are you?

JOSEPH'S BROTHERS. We are sons of Jacob, from a noble line.[46] We are twelve in all. Ten of us came to you. One brother remained behind to serve our father. A wolf devoured our younger brother. Our father loved him dearly, loved him best of all.

JOSEPH. You say "our father" is a prophet. Does a prophet act like this—some of his children he loves, some he does not? Such acts do not suit a prophet.

THE BROTHERS. Hear us out. You would have loved our brother too if you had seen him. We all loved him, our father most of all. But we were hateful to our brother. Believe us, that boy lied when he told his dreams to our father.

JOSEPH. What dreams did your brother have? How did your father interpret them?

THE BROTHERS. Our brother related strange dreams; Father interpreted them well, "All the wealth of Egypt will be yours." That's how he interpreted one of them.

JOSEPH. Your brother must have found happiness,[47] besides all the wealth of Egypt.

The brothers. No, a wolf ate him. But his soul must have gone to Heaven by now.

Now listen to what Joseph does. He gave his brothers grain; they took it and left. They cinched up their load. Without their knowing it, Joseph also returned what they had given him for the grain, had it concealed in their load.

Joseph, to his brothers. Once you get home, come back with your brother. I love you all. I follow the same religion as you. Go and return quickly. Don't forget your brother. When you come back, I will give you more grain.

Joseph's brothers' business was finished; they set out for home. Now the Devil returned. *Just see what he does.*

While the brothers were on their way back to Canaan, the Devil intercepted them. *Let me tell you what his intentions were. Hear me out. The Devil wished to leave his ugly smell on them. He wanted to wipe away the scent of Joseph. He wanted Jacob to go on weeping, day and night. If you believe in the Oneness of God, say prayers now so the Devil will go blind.*

When Joseph's brothers reached home, they were reunited with Jacob. They went straight to his house, sat down with him. As soon as Jacob saw them, he laughed. Then something came over him, he started to cry.

Joseph's brothers. Father, what is it? First you laughed, then you cried. What's come over you?

Jacob. When I first saw you, a sweet scent came to me. It made me laugh. I was happy. My heart was comforted. Then an ugly smell came to me. That's why I cried. Tell me, how did the lord of Egypt treat you? What is his religion?

Joseph's brothers. The lord of Egypt sends many greetings. He treated us royally, feasted us. He gave us much grain.

That sultan speaks beautifully. He professes Islam. He is a generous man. He constantly distributes bread to the poor. This is what he said to us. "Once you have returned home, bring your brother, come back again to Egypt. When I have laid eyes on him, I will know your intent. I will give you more grain."

When Jacob heard these words, he wept. Then he spoke to his sons.

JACOB. You took Joseph from me. You went off to the wilderness. You let a wolf have him. Now you want my other boy so you can take him away and do the same with him? I know it; you'll do with him as you did with Joseph.

JOSEPH'S BROTHERS. Father, we swear to you, all together. We'll watch over him. Nothing bad will happen to him, ever.

The brothers swore on their honor. Then they went and opened up their load. They found the cloth they had taken with them to Egypt. They saw it again there before their eyes.

JOSEPH'S BROTHERS. Father, these things of ours have been returned to us.

JACOB. He must not have liked the cloth. That's why he sent it back. Take it back with you. And don't let Benjamin out of your sight.

Be sure to bring him back. May God give you success in this business. Watch yourselves! Do not enter through one gate. Proclaim your faith loud and clear. Be careful! Remember, not through one gate all together.[48]

So Joseph's brothers set out again for Egypt. They kept close watch on Benjamin along the way. When they got to Egypt, they entered the city two by two.

Benjamin remained alone. *What else could he do? His father had given his brothers orders.*[49]

Shemdin, Joseph's son, stood watch at that one gate. Benjamin waited, he kept a respectful manner. *What did he know about the roads of the city? And how could those Egyptians understand him?* At that moment, Gabriel returned to Earth.

GABRIEL, TO JOSEPH. Your brothers have arrived. Take off your fine clothes, put on a coarse robe. Wrap a rough turban around your head.

Cover your face. Mount your camel. Your own brother cannot find his way. He has become separated from the rest. Get up now, take a camel and go to him. Bring your brother back here, to the palace. Shemdin will not grant him permission to enter. No one knows your brother's language.

Joseph mounted a camel and raced off. He went to Benjamin. *See what he says.* Joseph greeted him. Benjamin paid his respects in reply.

JOSEPH. Where are you from? Tell me, how did you get here?

BENJAMIN. I'm from Canaan. I came here with my brothers—ten of them in all. They went through the gate, two by two. They left me here. The gatekeeper doesn't understand me. But you do, so show me the way. And where did you learn my language?

JOSEPH. I traveled to Canaan when I was young. That's where I learned your language.

So Joseph spoke to Benjamin. He showed him the way, touched his arm. Then Joseph produced a bracelet and gave it to Benjamin. It was made of rubies, bright red. *How should I describe it? It was worth 12,000 pieces of Egyptian gold if you were to buy it.*

Benjamin took it. He had no idea of its worth. He thought the stones were glass; he did not want it. Joseph laughed.

Joseph. Put it on your arm. I'll take you to your brothers.

Then Joseph took him to a fine palace.

Joseph. You can relax here. Your brothers will come and find you. Now rest. Make yourself comfortable.

In time, Benjamin's brothers arrived. Joseph made them comfortable too.

Benjamin arose; he was overcome when he saw them. He moaned.

Benjamin's brothers. What's come over you? What's wrong? Why do you moan this way?

Benjamin. Such is the power of my God! A young man appeared, riding a camel. As soon as I saw him, I was relieved. He spoke Hebrew, gave me a bracelet. Look! When I saw him, my worries vanished. He came all this way with me.

Judah. Let me see the bracelet.

Benjamin gave Judah the bracelet. He too thought it was glass, put it on his own arm. The bracelet disappeared. Judah couldn't find it.

Benjamin. The bracelet came back to me. See, look at my arm.

No matter who got his hands on it, the bracelet always went back to Benjamin.

Now listen to Joseph, if you can follow my words.

Joseph ordered that a new palace be built. He had the likeness of Jacob drawn on one of its walls. He made the palace forty spans long and forty wide. Joseph had the likeness of each of Jacob's twelve sons drawn on those walls. Scene by scene, Joseph also had portrayed all those things his brothers had done to him—how they took him from their father, how they intended to kill him, how they took him from the well and sold him, how they put in writing his “three flaws,” how his brothers lied on that piece of paper.

Then Joseph called his brothers; he had them brought to his palace. They came, sat down. Wherever they looked, they saw what they had done to Joseph. They moaned; their hearts burned.

Joseph’s brothers, to each other. Those wicked things we did to Joseph, they’re all here.

When they looked at those pictures, their faces went pale, they trembled with fear.

Joseph ordered that bread and food be brought, had it set in front of them. Bravo! But none of the brothers could look at their food. They were all crying.

Joseph. You haven’t eaten.

His brothers. We’ve seen a portrait in this palace. We had a brother who looked just like that. He resembled that picture on the wall.

Everyone wept for him! A wolf devoured him. He has passed on to God. Looking at these pictures, we remembered him. That’s why we could not eat. Otherwise we could have gnawed on a stone we’re so hungry!

Joseph, to a servant. Take them to the other palace so they may eat their fill.

Joseph’s servants took the brothers to a different place. Joseph went with them. He ordered fine things be brought and set in front of each of them. They all ate, except for Benjamin. He could not contain himself.

Joseph, to Benjamin. Tell me, what’s the matter? Why do you cry? Your brothers have eaten, but still you sit here.

BENJAMIN. With your permission, I'll go. I could not eat while looking at those pictures. I had a brother—he looked like one of them. My brothers say he was eaten by a wolf. Let me torment myself with one last look at him. Let me brand my heart with the fire of longing. That's why I cry.

JOSEPH, TO HIS ATTENDANTS. Take him to that picture. He says he has a brother who looks just like it. Let him feast his eyes that he may be consoled. Gazing on that picture perhaps he will be calmed,[50] his tears will stop.

The attendants took Benjamin back to the palace where they had first been. Joseph went too. Benjamin entered the palace, sat down. He looked at the picture. Benjamin moaned.

JOSEPH, TO HIS SON. Mishelum, come here; let us talk. That man is your uncle. Go to him. He will see you and rejoice. If he asks, "Who is your father?" tell him the truth.

MISHELUM, TO BENJAMIN.[51] My father is Joseph, the mighty lord of Egypt.

When Benjamin heard these words, tears fell from his eyes.

MISHELUM. Why do you cry? Tell me!

BENJAMIN. I had a brother, Joseph. He looked like you. I did not know your father was my brother. My tears come from ignorance.

MISHELUM. Listen. Yes, my father is your brother. His name is Joseph; his father is Jacob, the prophet. They say that man has no equal in Canaan. He is the one who reunited you with your brother. He gave you a bracelet, you put it on your arm. He turned out to be your brother. You will meet with good fortune.

On hearing these words, Benjamin was overcome. Then he pulled himself together.

BENJAMIN. Where is that light of my eye? I was dead; now I am alive again. Come! Take me to him. Let me see his face. Where is he? Tell me.

MISHELUM. Be patient. I will go and tell your brother.

Mishelum informed his father. Joseph rose; he went to his meditation room.

JOSEPH, TO MISHELUM. Go, call Benjamin.

Mishelum did as Joseph commanded. When Benjamin entered the room and recognized his brother, he was overcome with joy. They talked and cried together. The angels saw them and were amazed.

JOSEPH. How is my father? What has become of him since we parted?

BENJAMIN. Why do you ask? Since you left he hasn't rested. He has wasted away with all his crying. His tears run like a river.

His beautiful eyes no longer see. He is beside himself. There is no life left in him. He can hardly stand up. All because of his grief over you. It goes on day and night. And your sister, Lady Dinah, she has not put on a decent gown for forty years.

JOSEPH. Brother, tell me, are you married? Do you have sons or daughters? What are their names?

BENJAMIN. I have three sons. I gave them names to remind me of you.

The first I named "Wolf," the second "Blood." The third I named "Joseph."

JOSEPH. Why those names? What were you thinking?

BENJAMIN. My brothers said, "Father, a wolf ate Joseph." They brought a bloody shirt to my father. He wept a long time, hoping God would grant him patience. For all his pain,

I named one son "Wolf," the same for the second son, "Blood." The third son I named "Joseph," not to forget you. That's why I named them.

Joseph. Benjamin, go to your brothers. But I warn you. I will conceal a measuring cup[52] in your sack. It's hidden in the grain. I'll call you a thief, I'll keep you from leaving.

Consoled at having found Joseph, Benjamin went to his brothers.

Now see what Joseph does. He covered his face,[53] went into the presence of his brothers. *In those days, it was the custom for a ruler to put on a veil in public.* Joseph ordered that food be brought. He had those with the same mother and father sit together. So they sat in pairs, except for Benjamin.

Joseph. Sit down, eat to your heart's content.

While all his brothers seated themselves, two by two, Benjamin remained by himself, alone.

Joseph. Let the ten brothers sit with each other. Benjamin, I will be brother to you, your companion.

When the brothers had finished their meal, they all applauded Joseph. *My words don't do it justice.* Then they prayed for Joseph.

Joseph had their loads made ready. He had the measuring cup concealed in Benjamin's sack.

The brothers set out on their return journey, applauding Joseph again. Joseph had his troops mount up. He gave them orders, sent them after his brothers.

Joseph, to his troops. A measuring cup is missing. Turn the caravan back now!

His troops mounted their horses. They headed off the caravan: "Stop, thieves!"

The brothers were forced to turn back, with deep misgiving.

The brothers. We stole no cup. We have never done a bad deed in our lives. We've done nothing wrong here. Give us an oath and we'll swear by it.

In those days, he who was guilty of theft did two years of hard labor.

After Joseph's men brought the brothers to the palace, they hobbled the camels. Joseph took his place on his throne; he had their sacks searched. The cup was found in Benjamin's sack. The brothers were petrified.

Joseph. I received you well, treated you better than the rest. I gave you wheat.

The brothers were shamed. They hung their heads. They stood there covering their faces.

The brothers. Listen to us. That boy is the rotten one. He had a brother, another thief, worse than us!

Now see where the story goes.

As a child Joseph had a nurse. For four years, she took care of him. She wouldn't let the child out of her sight. That nurse had a precious bead. She used to pin it to Joseph's sleeve. One day, the nurse brought Joseph to his father. She couldn't bear to be away from him. She decided to play a trick on Jacob.

The nurse. Jacob, where has your son gone? Bring him here. I had a priceless ruby bead. That boy of yours has made off with it. Hand him over.

Jacob went and found the boy.

Jacob. Joseph, where is your nurse's bead?

Joseph. I didn't take her bead. I haven't even seen it. Believe me.

Jacob searched Joseph; he found the bead on his arm.[54]

Jacob. Off with you, two years of labor.

They tell another story about Joseph. As a boy when he ate his meal, Joseph hid some of the food. He gave it to the needy. He fed both rich and poor. That's the reason his brothers said what they did, that Joseph was bad, that he was a thief.

Joseph considered his brothers. He thought to himself, "You're rotten, all of you. You torment your father. You sold your brother into slavery. Improperly gained, you kept the money."

Joseph was furious. He had Benjamin seized, ordered him put in prison. "Let him rot for two years!"

Joseph's brothers. Let Benjamin go! Take one of us instead. Don't take him! Don't make Jacob suffer any more. Have some respect for our father. We committed this crime. Don't keep Benjamin. Let him go.

Joseph. I'm not a tyrant. I don't jail the innocent. But the guilty will be punished. It is right to reproach the guilty, wrong to reproach the innocent.

The brothers put their heads together. "What shall we do?"

Judah. We must be prepared to make a sacrifice. Let's go to the marketplace, get arrows and swords. We can kill all these city people. We won't leave a man standing. Then we can take Benjamin and go home. Who can stop us!

That was Judah's way. With one shout from him, people were terrified, thousands would die.

But Joseph got reports; he spoke to his son, Mamil.

Joseph. Go to that man, put your hand on his waist. Rub his back.

Mamil did as he was told. Whatever strength Judah had, it drained away; his strength dried up. When Judah arose the next morning, his strength was gone.[55]

JUDAH'S BROTHERS. You didn't call out. You didn't crush those people after all!

JUDAH. Brothers, enough! A young man got hold of me, by my waist. I don't know who he was. What strength I had left me. I haven't been myself since then. Whoever he was, he must be one of the prophets.

While the brothers were commiserating, a man came to them from Joseph.

THE MAN. The mighty one summons you.

Joseph's brothers went, tears streaming down their faces.

JOSEPH. Twice you came. I received you with respect and generosity. You put your heads together, plotted to kill us. You weren't going to leave a man alive in this city. If you had seen me, you would have been unable to act.

Joseph was in a rage; he kicked the pavilion. The building nearly collapsed. Those who saw him were terrified.

JOSEPH. I hold your father in the highest regard, otherwise I would have crushed you all. I uncovered a thief among you and put the blame where it belongs. He is in prison. The rest of you can go. You have my leave.

The brothers bowed and left.

JUDAH. The rest of you go. I'll stay here. I won't leave Benjamin alone. When you get home, tell Father everything you've seen.

Joseph's brothers returned to Jacob in tears.

THE BROTHERS. Father, listen. They threw Benjamin in prison in Egypt—for robbery. Judah stayed behind with him. We've come back as we are. Look at us.

When Jacob heard their story, he could control himself no longer, he broke down.

Jacob. Did you see that man's face? Did you tell them Benjamin is no thief?

Joseph's brothers. We didn't see him clearly. He had darkened his eyes. We saw the cup come out of Benjamin's sack. If you don't believe us, ask the others in the caravan. They saw what happened, they'll tell you.

Jacob. I pray God will speed the time until I see them both again.

Joseph's brothers. Father, why do you speak this way? What do you mean!

Jacob. After difficulty comes respite. In my old age, I am weighed down with troubles. That is what I mean. God be my witness.

The Qur'an says, "Do not despair of God's comfort."[56] *Only an infidel would not believe these words.*

One day Azrail came to Earth. He came with God's command for Jacob, the prophet.

Jacob. Tell me, have you taken Joseph's soul?

Azrail. I have not taken his soul. I had no intention of taking his soul. Your son is alive. Do not imagine he is dead. He has become a powerful king in a foreign land. God has enabled your son to attain good fortune. Misfortune has turned to blessing.

Jacob. Tell me that I may know it.

Azrail. I have told you.

When he heard those words, Jacob prostrated himself in prayer, he gave thanks. Then he raised his head saying, "I grieve for Joseph."[57]

Jacob. Benjamin, light of my eyes, where are you? Come to me! And Joseph, my heart's desire, fruit of my loins, the one who is out of my sight, partner to my Benjamin, my precious lamb. If only every worthless conceit of mine could be a sacrifice for you. "Joseph," your name is always on my lips. Whenever I speak your name, my heart is engulfed in fire. In this world, my longing is for you alone. I fear I will never see you again, my beloved boy.

As he spoke, Jacob found inner consolation. Then he lost consciousness, collapsed.

Jacob's sons. Father, you waste yourself with your tears, never letting go of Joseph. Give up your hope. Stop talking about him. Take care of yourself. Stop crying.

Jacob. I will not give up hope, ever. I appeal to my Lord: "May the day come when I see the face of Joseph again, when he will speak and I will hear his sweet voice again."

Then and there Jacob reproved his sons.

Jacob. Where is there anyone like you! God gave you strength that he gave to none other. You left that boy rotting in prison. You failed to bring him back from Egypt. Had Judah just once exerted himself, just once called out! Had you once struck a blow, frightened those people, you could have rescued Benjamin! If I could only see his face, how I would rejoice.

Joseph's brothers. Father, believe us. Trust what we say. We saw men there stronger than us. We were afraid. We didn't resist, we couldn't say a word.

Jacob. Bring me my pen. Let me put my pain down in words, I'll make it clear. Call Simeon, have him come. I'll tell my woes to him, have him write them down, one after the other.

They brought Jacob pen and ink. Simeon came.

Simeon. Father, what do you desire? What is your command? Tell me and I will write it down.

Jacob. First, recall His name.[58] Then describe my desolation. "From me, Jacob, to that mighty Ruler of Egypt." Write him a letter. Let's see how he replies. Now write. Tell him of my circumstances, describe my endless suffering—how I am forever beside myself. Put that down. Say I have gone blind from weeping. Because of that, tell him, I am consumed by this fire of separation. I am broken by my losses. Spell out to him the pain I feel. Tell him about my son who was devoured by the wolf. "His brother is the one you have thrown in prison. He is the only one now who can console my heart. He is the one you have detained." Write that down. "A prophet does not steal, he does not take what is not his." Say that. In truth, this charge against Benjamin is a lie. They are all slaves. That mighty Lord is Sultan. His rule prevails. What He desires, He does. May he confirm my words and trust them! Trusting my words, may he give back my son. Respecting me, may he gladden my heart. Otherwise I shall pray to God, with much weeping, that calamity should befall that mighty ruler. That sultan commanded his servants. He bid them hide that cup in Benjamin's sack.

Jacob finished his dictation, "Now I wish for you eternal prosperity. I send greetings of peace. Do not detain my son and cause me grief. Do not make me groan day and night. Send my son back to me! Let him return! Endless good prayers to you."

So Jacob had Simeon put his words in writing. *Now listen to what he does.* Jacob commanded his sons.

Jacob. Go. Take this letter to that mighty ruler. Give it to him. When you arrive, pay your respects. Kiss his hands!

Jacob's sons arose. They set out once again. When they reached Egypt, they bowed down before that king in respectful submission. Presenting Jacob's letter, they kissed their brother's hands. Joseph accepted the letter. He kissed it, pressed it to his eyes. Then he spoke to them all.

JOSEPH. Do you know why I kissed this letter? I love your father very much.

JOSEPH'S BROTHERS. This is the custom of a ruler. If a letter arrives from an upright one, he kisses it.

Joseph opened the letter, had it read. Tears poured down his cheeks.

JOSEPH, TO HIS TREASURER. Go to the treasury. Bring me the chest.

The treasurer did as he was told; he returned with the chest.

Joseph opened it. *Now hear what he does.* He removed a piece of writing from the chest. He showed it to his brothers, handed it over to them.

JOSEPH. Read!

Joseph wanted to hear from them everything that was written on it.

Everything that Joseph's brothers had done to him—how they had sold Joseph, how they had spoken of "three faults"—all of that was written clearly. Listen to what Joseph does to them.

Joseph's brothers took the writing. They passed it among themselves, looked at each other.

JOSEPH. What sort of writing is this! Tell me so I may know what to think of it.

JOSEPH'S BROTHERS. This is a strange document. We don't understand. The writing is bad. We can't grasp its meaning.

JOSEPH. It seems you sold a boy. It seems you wrote, "He has three faults."

Joseph's brothers were tongue-tied, their faces grew pale. Their wits abandoned them. They were feverish with fear.

Joseph's brothers. We never sold a slave like this. We never wrote something like this. We have no idea about any of this. We cannot speak about something we do not understand.

Joseph. Bring me the cup. Whichever of you wrote this, let the cup speak to you.

They brought the cup. Joseph rose. He struck the cup once with a gold coin.

Joseph. Sons of Jacob, how pleasing are the words of this cup. It speaks of things that have come to pass. Marvel at its creator.

Through His power, it speaks to us. Can you reply? We will ask it a question.

Joseph's brothers. We are ready. *What will it say? Now see what Joseph does with that coin!*

Joseph struck the coin against the cup. The cup rang. It revealed its inmost secrets.

Joseph. The cup tells me strange things!

Joseph's brothers. We will believe the cup. Let it speak. Tell us what that cup has to say.

Joseph. Listen to the cup's words, how they reveal its secret truth!

The cup. These ten brothers took Joseph from his father. They went out for a walk.

Joseph. Is it true what the cup says, what it says about you?

Joseph's brothers. The cup speaks the truth. You knew. *Now pay attention.*

Again Joseph struck the cup. Again the cup rang, let out a sound.

JOSEPH. It seems[59] you took the boy's bread. Is it true? It seems you removed his shirt. And in the end, it seems you dropped him in a well, buried him. It seems you left him for dead.

JOSEPH'S BROTHERS. It is the truth. What the cup has said, it is all true.

JOSEPH. It seems you were going to kill the boy, but the eldest among you saved him; it seems he did not let you kill Joseph. Listen to the cup again.

Again Joseph struck the cup. *Listen; what does Joseph say?*

JOSEPH. He was your elder, an example for you. You cannot say this cup has lied. His name was Judah, your eldest brother. The cup has revealed this clearly to me. It seems you left the boy in a well, then sold him for a slave, unlawfully!

JOSEPH. These are all your deeds. You sold your brother claiming he was a slave. Shamelessly, not fearing God, you made a false contract.

And then you say, "We are from a line of prophets." Everything you do is like this. Why do you lie so boastfully? In the end, liars will only burn in Hell!

Joseph ordered that his brothers be bound.

JOSEPH. Kill them all. Hang them from a tree until they die!

Joseph terrified his brothers. They beseeched him for mercy.

JOSEPH'S BROTHERS. One of us has already vanished. Our father, Jacob, has gone blind. What will become of him when he can no longer see the rest of us? He will surely give up the ghost.

They all wept. *As for Joseph, listen.*

Joseph's heart ached for his brothers. At that moment, he revealed his face to them. With that he opened their eyes. He sprinkled rose water over them. When they beheld Joseph's face, they were overcome with grief. Their limbs trembled in awe at the sight of him. *How shall we put it?* Joseph's brothers consoled one another.

Joseph. I am your brother, Joseph. My Creator made me a powerful ruler.

When that Righteous One, the son of Jacob, uttered these words, his brothers hung their heads. They recalled their evil deeds.

Joseph's brothers. Brother, forgive us. Pardon our errors. Speak well of us. Give thanks. You have become powerful, a great ruler. Forgive us!

Joseph. I have forgiven you, pardoned your sins. I have treated you well. Come. Let us embrace one another. Let us relax and sit together, enjoy each other's company.

Joseph and his brothers sat down together. Their hearts were at peace.

Joseph. Now, what is to be done? First I must send my shirt to Jacob. Take it to him so he may rejoice. Perhaps then he will be free of his tears. Ask him to pardon your sins. Perhaps then he will forgive you.

Here is a question for you. Why did Joseph give them his shirt to take? He did not give them his handkerchief or his ring! "Take my shirt," he commanded. Here is the answer. But first, with all sincerity invoke blessings on the prophet.

When Joseph went down into the well, he was naked. Remember, Gabriel brought him a shirt, put it around him. This is the garment that Joseph sent now. Anyone who put it on would be protected from illness. No harm would come to any of his limbs. Were a troubled person to put on that shirt, his troubles would vanish. If a man at peace put it on, imagine what he could do! That was why Joseph sent the shirt, not his ring or handkerchief.

JOSEPH. My father's sightless eyes will see once more.

There is another story here. Perhaps it will please you to hear it. When Joseph's mother died, see what his father did. The day Rachel died Jacob took a concubine. Now that woman already had a child named Beshir.[60] She was still nursing that boy. *Let me tell you what happened.* Jacob sold Beshir, the woman's son, so she would have enough milk for Joseph.

JACOB'S CONCUBINE, TO HER CREATOR. Lord, Jacob has taken my child from me, separated me from the one I love. He makes me suffer day and night.

A VOICE FROM THE UNSEEN. I have accepted your prayer. Do not worry. You will see your son again and rejoice. I will reunite you with him. Then I will reunite Jacob with his son.

THE WOMAN. I will make Jacob cry. May he go blind! May he never leave his place of suffering!

That was the reason Jacob cried, why he moaned for Joseph day and night.

Many years passed. A merchant sold Beshir to Joseph. Joseph held Beshir in high regard, above all the rest. Every task that Joseph gave him, Beshir carried through to completion.

It was Beshir now to whom Joseph gave his shirt, to take and give to Jacob. Joseph also wrote a letter that he gave to Beshir to take with the garment.

JOSEPH. Take these to Canaan; give them to Jacob.

Beshir took the shirt and left. *Now offer prayers; I'll tell you what happens.*

When Beshir was still ten days distant from Canaan, God gave the wind permission to blow. *That's how Joseph's scent reached Jacob. God's intent was for Jacob to smile, just once.*

JACOB. Look, the scent of Joseph comes to my nose. I'll spread the news that he must be alive!

JACOB'S GRANDSONS. Grandfather, when will Joseph's scent ever leave your nose? It's the scent of your servant that you're smelling. That's what you smell. Steam rises from your soul.[61]

Beshir reached Canaan, saw an old woman washing clothes. Beshir greeted her; she accepted his greetings. He said a few words to that woman.

BESHIR. Tell me, where is the house of Jacob? Speak up!

THE WOMAN. Jacob is in great pain.

BESHIR. I bring a letter from Joseph. I come with good news for Jacob.

When the woman heard those words, her eyes filled with tears.

THE WOMAN. God, You vowed, You made a promise to Your wretched slave—"First I will reunite you with your son. Then I will bring Jacob together with Joseph." Now a bearer of good tidings has come from Joseph. My grief only increases. I will burst with rage. And still my son has not come home. Hearing this news, I am distraught.

BESHIR. Woman, who are you? What are you talking about? Speak up!

THE WOMAN. I will tell you my story. God gave me a son, but Jacob sold him. Jacob made me suffer. To this day, I have not stopped crying. My son's name is Beshir. He has a beautiful name and he is of good character.

Beshir. But I am that one you call "son." I am the one you just described.

On hearing Beshir's words, the woman crumbled in a heap. She hadn't the strength to stand or collect her wits. For a time she lay on the ground; then she pulled herself together, stood up, only to collapse again, calling out, "My son."

Finally mother and son were tearfully reunited. *If you had seen them, you would scarcely have believed your eyes.* The woman took Beshir's hand. She took him to Jacob. *Listen now to Jacob.*

Beshir greeted Jacob; he gave him Joseph's shirt. Jacob took it, rubbed it on his face. Jacob's eyes were opened; he could see again.

Jacob. Who are you? You have brought news of my son. You speak well, you brought me this shirt. When I rubbed it on my face, my eyes opened. Seeing you I rejoice!

Beshir. Listen to me. I am the one you made an orphan. You took me away from my mother, sold me. You said, "Let Joseph suck her milk." You sold me and made me an orphan.

Jacob. I never knew the fire of separation could be like this. Now I have known it myself. Didn't I tell you! Joseph's scent has finally reached us.

So Jacob embraced Beshir; he kissed him. Jacob opened the shirt that Beshir had brought. He removed the letter. He opened it and read. As he spoke, Jacob drove out the name of the Devil with the name of God.

If you give me your ear I will tell you what was in that letter.

It was written thus: "From me, Joseph, to you, Jacob. Greetings, Father, a thousand times over! I am your son, Joseph. I have become a mighty ruler in Egypt. When this letter reaches you, give thanks to God, day and night. May He allow me to see the object of my longing! He has the power to make this happen."

Jacob heard these words of Joseph. He prostrated himself, gave thanks to God.

Now hear what Joseph does. In Egypt, Joseph gave orders to his brothers. He gave them countless robes, strings of horses, mules, and camels.

Joseph. Take these animals; go quickly. Get my father. Bring them all here. Leave no one behind.

Jacob's sons journeyed back to their father. They gathered all around him.

Jacob's sons. We are the ones who took Joseph. We are the ones who sold him as a slave. God has made him a mighty ruler in Egypt. Now we bring you news of him. Pardon us. We have committed sins. Do not punish us.

Jacob. I forgive your sins. I treat you now with compassion. I have done right by you. May the Pardoner have mercy on you too. May He accept these words from me, Jacob, his servant.

In that same hour, Gabriel came.

Gabriel. Jacob, the Illustrious One has commanded you, "Arise now, go and embrace the one you have longed for."

Jacob. Thanks be to God, day and night.

Jacob collected his sons, his slaves, all his retinue. After many days,[62] they reached Egypt.

In Egypt, Joseph and his soldiers, left and right, all mounted up. They went out the distance of a day's journey from the city to greet Jacob.

Joseph dismounted; he greeted his father. They proceeded on foot together toward the city.

Joseph's nurse cried when she greeted him. All who saw them were astonished. On reaching Egypt, they all rejoiced, gave thanks for being reunited. Then Joseph commanded the Egyptians to gather together. Rich and poor, Joseph addressed them all.

JOSEPH. Come. Tell me who you are! Whose slaves are you?

THE EGYPTIANS. We are all your slaves.

JOSEPH. Showing thanks to God, I free you now. Because I am reunited with my father, I have freed you all.

Seventy years had passed since father and son had been separated.

Now seventy years later they came together again. *Others say it was forty years that passed before Jacob found Joseph.*

Moral

An anecdote comes to mind here. Offer prayers that your sins may be pardoned.

When Joseph saw his father, he set free his slaves. To honor his father he freed them all.

God too will act beneficently at the end of time. Then He will pardon His slaves. When the Day of Resurrection arrives, all His creatures will be gathered together in that place. Listen! Muhammad's community, whoever they are, wherever they are, the followers of that Most Laudable One, hope of sinners, they will all be brought into God's presence by His command. God will ask those Muslims, "Whose slave are you? Now is the time for you to speak." They will reply, "We are all Your slaves." And God will say, "I have freed you. I have pardoned your sins. I have forgiven you for the sake of Muhammad, that Most Laudable One, Pride of the Here and Hereafter."

Now listen, I will tell you about those sons of Joseph.

Jacob. Who are those young men? Tell me! What is their relation to you?

Joseph. Father, they are my sons, my children, by Zeliha.

And Jacob gave thanks for that.

Now Jacob wished to see Zeliha. He wished to meet her, talk with her, get to know her.

Jacob. Have her servants call Zeliha. Bring her here so I may see her.

A servant went and brought Zeliha. So Jacob saw her, got to know her. He understood Zeliha's heart was pure. Then Zeliha spoke to Joseph.

Zeliha. I shall honor your father. Allow me to invite him to the palace.

Joseph. He is a prophet; he would not find such luxury proper. You may invite him if you wish. But have a modest home built for him, something small and humble. Build a house like the one in Canaan. Make your invitation, then have him as your guest. He will be comfortable in a house like that.

They had a house like that made for Jacob. Then they called him. Jacob went; he was astonished at what Joseph had done. "He had this one made just like my own home, in Canaan!" So Jacob sent out word to his own people.

Jacob settled in his new house. Zeliha brought him fine food.

Jacob. I've lived to 120 but I never ate such food. A prophet does not eat like this.

Altogether Jacob remained in Egypt forty years. Then Gabriel descended from heaven. He greeted Jacob.

Gabriel. Jacob, it is time to go, time for Azrail to come and take your soul. This land of Egypt is not your home. Go, be with your father.

Jacob, to Joseph. My son, this land of Egypt is not my home. Gabriel came to me. He said, "Azrail will come for you soon. Prepare yourself. Go, be with your father. From now on your place is there." That was his command. I am going now from your city. You too leave this city behind.

So Jacob took ten sons and set out for Canaan. In time he reached his home. One day, Jacob went to the grave of his father. He saw angels there, digging a fresh grave. Jacob approached them, he greeted them.

Jacob. What is this grave? For whom are you digging it?

The angels. God sent us. He said, "One of Our friends is going to die." That's why we came to dig this grave. We have told you because you asked.

As the angels finished digging the grave, Jacob's soul hastened to take its leave. Jacob was impatient; he wished to enter the grave. Orchards and vineyards of Paradise appeared before his eyes. *How can I explain how much Jacob's soul longed for it!*

The angels. Don't hurry!

One angel[63] held out a goblet full of wine, presented it to Jacob: "Drink!" The angel offered Jacob the goblet so his soul might fly away and leave his body. Jacob took the goblet saying, "In the name of God." Jacob drank the wine. Then, giving up his soul, his body fell to the ground.

The angels washed Jacob's body then and there. His eleven sons were present. They wrapped Jacob in a shroud, took his body, and laid it down beside Isaac. *Let no one ask, "Where is Jacob's body?"*

The graves of four people are there. One is Abraham, the second Isaac, third is Sarah, and the fourth, Jacob. Four fortunate ones rest there,[64] each one more radiant than the others.

Now listen. I will tell you about Jacob's sons, what they did.

Jacob's sons went back to Joseph, overcome with grief.

Jacob's sons. Our father has died.

Joseph heard the news and wept. He was beside himself with grief.

"Let us die in submission; unite me with the righteous."[65]

At that hour, Gabriel descended from heaven. He brought greetings from the Lord. He spoke to Joseph.

Gabriel. You have sixty months until you reach the term of your own life. When your time comes, your life will end. Of that there is no doubt. The call to Prophethood has come to you, Joseph. Arise! Call the people to you, inform them!

Joseph called the people, invited them to the true faith. He destroyed the churches, smashed those crosses. The news of Joseph's actions reached King Reyyan. *It was the habit of the infidels to build churches.*

Reyyan. Joseph, give up this business. The people of Egypt do not believe in your faith. Do not speak to them of it. They will not listen. Leave the people to their accustomed ways. Do not try to call them to your religion.

Joseph, to Reyyan. I call the people to the straight path. If they do not come I shall rain destruction upon them. Now I will leave the city, take my leave of its people. You will see what I shall do to them.

Joseph, to his people. Gather together. Each one of you, build a house outside the city.

Joseph gathered his own brothers. They left the city with him.

They built their houses outside the city. Those who accepted the true faith joined them.

At that place that Jacob had reached when he was first reunited with Joseph, away from the Nile, Joseph and his brothers laid the foundations of a great city. Joseph named it the City of Faiyum. They built it on both sides of the river. They called that place Haremeyn.[66]

That new city was filled with blessings. All who saw it were dazzled by its greatness; they were filled with desire. King Reyyan also wished to see it. He sought permission from Joseph to go there.

Joseph. No infidel shall come here; none shall enter this city. Let the king become a Muslim and accept our faith. Let him be free of doubt and hesitation. Then he may come and enter this city. May God make him successful in all his deeds.

When King Reyyan heard these words, he accepted Joseph's faith. *No doubt, unbelief falls away and is forgiven.*

The king accepted the true faith; he entered that city. Seeing it all, he could scarcely believe his eyes.

Then Joseph rejoiced; he grew old. The time was near when his life, too, would end. He called his eldest son to bid him farewell.

Joseph. Protect your religion! Guard your faith!

Zeliha preceded Joseph in death. Joseph wept for her. 1500
Before any time at all had passed, Joseph too departed this
world. He yielded up his soul to God. He abandoned the physi-
cal world. His sons and brothers gathered together. They made
a coffin there for Joseph. They washed his body and wrapped
him in a shroud, clean and pure. They put Joseph in a coffin
and prayed. They sent the coffin outside the city.

Now none of Egypt's crops grew, nor any of its grasses. 1505
There was terrible famine throughout Egypt. King Reyyan sent
an envoy to Joseph's sons with his demand.

THE KING'S ENVOY. Raise the coffin! Bring it to our side! Let Joseph remain with us. If you refuse, I shall come and wreak havoc on you.

Joseph's sons consulted among themselves. Let us raise the coffin. Let us take Joseph back to Egypt.[67]

And so they did. This time terrible scarcity followed on the
other side of the river. They consulted with the king. They 1510
placed the coffin in the middle of the river. On either side of
the river, there was famine, they say; the city itself was filled
with blessing. For a long time, the coffin stayed hidden in the
water. Now Joseph's sons had become orphans.

Listen to what happens next. I will tell you about the Prophet Moses.

GOD, TO MOSES. Go! Find Joseph and remove his body
from those waters. You must reunite Joseph with Jacob. Do 1515
this now.

Moses came to Egypt. He looked for the coffin but could not find it. He did not know where Joseph's body was. And an old woman saw him there.

The old woman. Moses, I will tell you where Joseph's coffin is if you will show compassion toward me on the Day of Resurrection, that day when all the people will cry out. May God spare me then from the fire of Hell.

Moses. Tell me where to find the coffin, and I will intercede for you on that day.

The woman showed Joseph's coffin to Moses, knowing he would intercede for her on the Day of Resurrection. Moses took the coffin and left. He had it sent to Jacob's own resting place. *Now see what Moses does.* He had it placed outside the door.[68] He left it there. That is where Joseph's bones lie.

Now I will end my story here. Let us invoke blessings from God on that most laudable one. I have made a summary account of this story for those who will hear it. Let them offer a prayer for the one who turned it into verses. God, do not hold the versifier of this story responsible for his sins. Lord, Sheyyad Hamza is your lowly slave. Pardon his sins. Have mercy on the one who put this story in verse and on those who listen to it.

[And make your pardon a blessing also for the one who put this copy down on paper.]

Notes

1. "His": While Turkish does not recognize gender, Arabic does. In the latter language, Allah, grammatically at least, is considered masculine (l. 0001).

2. "houris . . . like the moon": A round, radiant face was an ideal type of beauty for Muslim poets. Houris are believed to await believers in paradise (l. 0008).

3. Lady Dinah: Hamza calls her Jacob's stepdaughter. In the biblical story, she is Jacob's own daughter, by Leah, and so Joseph's half-sister. She is not mentioned at all in the Qur'an (l. 0061).

4. "The Voice": Here the agent of the command is not named. In several other lines, Hamza uses a Turkish word (*ün*) together with its source (explicitly "God") or an Arabic word (*hatif*) suggesting an unseen place above (l. 0102).

5. "a big tree": See below, l. 0671, note 35 (l. 0132).

6. *"there is another saying"*: Hamza points to variant exegetical tradition (l. 0136).

7. "up out of my collar": This may be an allusion to commentary on sura liv, 1 of the Qur'an ("the moon was split in two") according to which part of the moon came out of Muhammad's collar. See also introduction, n. 28 (l. 0169).

8. "Beshir": The (Arabic) name means "bringer of glad tidings"; it derives from a verb used in the Qur'anic narrative. The character, however, is not named there (l. 0187).

9. "It is I": While not literally spoken by Joseph, these words should be understood as his expression of astonishment on seeing himself in "the mirror" (l. 0195).

10. "He's a thief": See ll. 1152ff. (l. 0214).

11. "renounced his brotherhood": It would have been illegal for Joseph's brothers to sell a free man into slavery (l. 0228).

12. "the grave of Joseph's mother": Rachel is traditionally believed to have been buried along a road near Bethlehem (l. 0235).

13. "Banyas" [?]: The reading of the manuscript is uncertain. Banyas is traditionally associated with the house of Jacob and the well of Joseph. A less likely reading is "Baysan," the Hebrew "Be't She'an." The early thirteenth-century pilgrim Ali al-Harawi comments on both places. See Josef W. Meri, trans., *A Lonely Wayfarer's Guide to Pilgrimage* (Princeton, NJ: Darwin Press, 2004): 40 and 42, respectively, and the map on p. 10. A still less likely reading would be the biblical Beth-el (the Arab, later Palestinian village of Beytin). It was the site of a famous dream of Jacob's, an incident not referred to in the Joseph story (l. 0258).

14. "Nablus": the ancient Neapolis; identified with the biblical Shechem (l. 0267).

15. "Jerusalem": The route of the merchant and his caravan should be read as a suggestive, not literal itinerary (l. 0269).

16. "Arish": Al-'Arish, situated near the Mediterranean coast at the northern extremity of the Sinai peninsula, was on a well-used caravan route between Egypt and Palestine. Ibn Battuta stayed overnight there on a journey around 1326 (l. 0290).

17. "Egypt": Ḥamza does not distinguish between the country and its chief city, using "Mısır" to stand for both (l. 0301).

18. "Jonah": For Jonah's encounter with the whale, see Qur'an, sura xxxvii, 139ff. (l. 0322).

19. "Solomon": He is mentioned in several chapters of the Qur'an; the story of the theft and recovery of his ring is a later development in Muslim narrative tradition. Cf. *Tha'labi*, 537–44, or *Kisa'i*, 300–301 (l. 0322).

20. "mighty one" (*aziz*): In Zeliha's dream, Joseph calls himself by the noun used in the Qur'an (xii, 30) of the Egyptian ruler (l. 0342).

21. "a righteous man" (*siddik*): An epithet used for Joseph (l. 0399).

22. "The sultan": The title Hamza reserves for Qutayfar (l. 0407).

23. "put kohl around them": Hamza's wording is ambiguous. He may describe Zeliha's adorning herself or further explain the picture she has just drawn (l. 0480).

24. "the Devil" (*Iblis*): His refusal to follow God's command, at the time of Creation, and to bow down and worship the newly fashioned Adam led to his being reviled (l. 0506).

25. *"Tomorrow":* Hamza refers to the Day of Judgment (l. 0512).

26. *"Do not despair . . ."* (Arabic): Q xxxix, 53 (l. 0517).

27. "Fear the day . . ." (Arabic): Q ii, 281 (l. 0522).

28. "And thou shall not . . ." (Arabic): Q xvii, 32 (l. 0534).

29. *"And whoever does"* (Arabic): Q xcix, 8. Hamza quotes only the first words of the verse, completing the sentence in Turkish paraphrase. The preceding words ("See what it says"), which I take to be the narrator's, could also be Joseph speaking to Zeliha, another example of the poet's seamless transitions (l. 0541).

30. "through his fingers": Sexual innuendo seems obvious here (l. 0545).

31. "This is no mortal" (Arabic): Q xii, 31 (l. 0592).

32. "took off his robe": Zeliha took off Joseph's ceremonial robe (see above, lines 420ff.; l. 0602).

33. "Speak! . . . Speak!": In Gabriel's command to Joseph (repeated four times in three lines), we may hear an echo of God's command ("Say!") to Muhammad in the Qur'an. See, for example, the opening lines of suras cix, cxii, cxiii, and cxiv (l. 0648).

34. "a stranger" (*garib*): Hamza uses a word that not only means a person away from his homeland, but that has the connotation of someone separated from (and longing for) God, a term much used by Turkish mystics (l. 0668).

35. "a very big tree": In *Tha'labi* we read, "the beginning of the affair of Joseph and Jacob . . . was that God made a tree for Jacob in the courtyard of his house. Each time a son was born to him, God would make a new branch" (*Tha'labi*, 185). Cf. also above (l. 0132): "There was a big tree by the road" (l. 0671).

36. "His face was covered": There is no reason for Joseph, here in prison, to be hidden. Hamza's comment suggests a Muslim aversion to pictorial representation of the human face, especially that of Muhammad, his family members, or other pre-Islamic prophets. For examples of such veiling in sixteenth-century Ottoman art, see Emel Esin, *Turkish Miniature Painting* (Rutland, VT: Charles E. Tuttle, 1960), plates 4–7; see also ll. 1129–30 (l. 0692).

37. "the wine steward": This is the same person, by another name, as the "cupbearer" (l. 0710).

38. *"oleander":* This poisonous tree is mentioned a number of times in the Qur'an (e.g., sura xxxvii, 62), where it is identified as a source of food for dwellers in Hell (l. 0781).

39. *"Malik":* One of the "keepers" of Hell, mentioned in Q xliii, 76 (l. 0782).

40. *"Sea of Living Creatures":* Compare Tha'labi's account of the Creation where he refers to the "seventh heaven [in which] there is a sea of light

called al-Hayawan [Living Creatures], which Gabriel enters every morning" (*Tha'labi*, 27; l. 0800).

41. *"Oh, Lord, grant us . . .":* A slight variation on Q iii, 194 (l. 0846).

42. *"What that Generous One promises He fulfills"* (Arabic): The source of this saying is unknown to me (l. 0848).

43. "Fourteen sons": The Qur'anic story mentions neither a marriage to the Egyptian woman nor any children. According to later Muslim tradition, going back to Genesis, Joseph had only two sons, Manassah and Ephraim (l. 0918).

44. "Mamil": The coincidence of giving this son the same name as that of one of the merchant's slaves (above, l. 0187) is unexplained (l. 0920).

45. Lines 0936–43: omitted; see introduction, n. 40.

46. "noble line" (*şerif*): Hamza uses a word applied to the family and descendants of Muhammad (l. 0972).

47. "found happiness": This strikes a rare note of irony in Hamza's poem (l. 0983).

48. "not through one gate all together": An allusion to Q xii, 67. And see the following note (l. 1022).

49. *"His father . . . orders":* Joseph's construction of the "network" of roads (l. 0924), an act contrary to the Qur'an's story, created an obstacle to his brothers entering the city by different gates, as commanded by Jacob. Their entering "two by two" reflects a different narrative tradition and serves to highlight Benjamin's isolation (l. 1025).

50. "perhaps he will be calmed": Joseph speaks here with a rational, sober voice and suggests that the image of his lost brother will console Benjamin. Like Zeliha before him, however, Benjamin is portrayed as desiring, rather, to increase his suffering (l. 1088).

51. "MISHELUM": A line containing Benjamin's implied question (as just imagined by Joseph) has presumably been lost (l. 1094).

52. "measuring cup": In Genesis (xliv, 2) and in some later traditions, the object is said to be a precious drinking goblet (l. 1127).

53. "covered his face": While rulers sometimes did conceal their identity in public (as Hamza says in the next line), Joseph's doing so here would have been to preserve his anonymity. Joseph's behavior would have been

more appropriate on his first appearing before his brothers (l. 1129). See also above, l. 0692, n. 36.

54. "found the bead on his arm": The story parallels Benjamin's situation (l. 1163).

55. "his strength was gone": The parallel with the angel's rubbing Joseph's back (l. 0545) is striking (l. 1183).

56. *"Do not despair"* (Arabic): Q xii, 87 (l. 1211).

57. "I grieve for Joseph" (Arabic): Q xii, 84 (l. 1219).

58. "recall His name": See the discussion in the introduction about invoking the name of God (l. 1242).

59. "It seems": The Turkish language's inferential or narrative past tense becomes a subtle grammatical tool in Joseph's formulations here of his brothers' actions: he feigns ignorance of them despite having been victim of all of them (l. 1295).

60. "Beshir": He presumably has the same name as the merchant's slave who helped pull Joseph from the well because he plays a similar, annunciatory role in the story (l. 1339).

61. "Steam rises from your soul": Jacob's passionate preoccupation with Joseph is here seen from a mystical point of view. Cf. the fiery heat of Zeliha's breath at l. 0900 (l. 1358).

62. "After many days": Literally, "73 days" (l. 1405).

63. "One angel": That is, Azra'il, the Angel of Death. For a very different view of how the angel took life away in Turkish folk belief of the time, see Lewis, *The Book of Dede Korkut*, 111 (l. 1462).

64. "Four fortunate ones rest there": Sarah was Jacob's first wife. By "there" Hamza, following Muslim and Jewish tradition, presumably means Hebron (l. 1469).

65. "Let us die . . . with the righteous" (Arabic): Q xii, 101 (l. 1473).

66. "City of Faiyum . . . Haremeyn": Hamza's description is clarified by the corresponding passage in *Kisa'i* (191): Joseph "excavated a branch of the Nile and called it the Faiyum. On the banks of the river he built edifices and constructed two cities, which he called al-Haramayn," two holy places (l. 1488).

67. "back to Egypt": i.e., the ancient city where Joseph first ruled (l. 1508).

68. "outside the door": Muslim tradition places Joseph's tomb either at Hebron or Nablus. Ibn Battuta placed the grave in a mosque at Hebron. To his translation at this point, Gibb added, "The putative tomb of Joseph is now shown in a separate exterior chapel" (*Travels of Ibn Battuta* 1: 75 n. 23). For a plan of the relevant structures in Hebron, see the article "Machpelah" in *EJ*, xiii, 325–27 (l. 1522).

Afterword

Hamza's "Story of Joseph" was composed in a language called Old Anatolian (or Old Ottoman) Turkish, from which the language of modern Turkey evolved. Turkish belongs to the Turkic language group, which includes languages like Uzbek, Kirghiz, Turkmen, and Uyghur, with large numbers of speakers from Europe to northeast Asia. That group in turn is a member of the Altaic language family, making it (in the view of many) a relative of the Mongol and Tunguz language groups. Some scholars believe "Proto Turkic" was related to Korean or Japanese, or both.[1] As an Altaic language, Old Anatolian Turkish was structurally different from both Arabic and Persian, members, respectively, of the Semitic and Indo-European language families.

The oldest surviving examples of a Turkish language ("Old Turkic")—apart from isolated words cited in Chinese and Byzantine sources—date from the eighth century CE. They are in the form of inscriptions on funerary stones (stele) carved in so-called runic (or "runiform") characters.[2] These monumental stones, celebrating the deeds of early Turkish rulers, are found in the Orkhon and Yenisey river valleys, north of the Altai mountain range in what is today Mongolia, an area generally accepted as the oldest historic Turkish homeland. In terms of content, these inscriptions are also the earliest surviving examples of Turkish narrative.

Speakers of Old Turkic mostly practiced pastoral nomadism and, although the evidence is sparse, probably followed animistic or shamanistic religious practices. But that language and that cultural setting would already have seemed archaic in Hamza's time.[3]

While the Inner Asian homeland of the Turkish-speaking peoples lay north of the Altai mountains, the important regions controlled by their earliest empires lay further south, astride ancient caravan routes that connected the Mediterranean world to China. These routes, later to be known collectively as the "Silk Road," facilitated not only trade but the exchange of ideas and religions. Over the course of time, especially from the time of their earliest steppe (Kök Türk) empire, Turks were exposed to and sometimes adopted the beliefs and practices of those several communities of faith—Buddhism, Zoroastrianism, Manichaeism, Judaism, and Christianity (primarily in its Nestorian form)—that were represented in Inner Asia. Turkish conversion to the teachings of those major historical religions of Eurasia is documented not only by reports of successful missionaries, foreign emissaries, and others but by writings of the new converts themselves, in Old Turkic but mostly in other alphabets.[4]

Those religious texts (primarily Buddhist, Manichaean, and Christian), now scattered and often fragmentary, provide a record—however partial—of the impact that those religions had on Turkish speakers across Central Asia. Conversely, it is those texts that, excepting the inscriptions of the stele, account for the bulk of writing in Old Turkic, only very broadly what we would call literature. An educated elite largely monopolized literacy, and in a pre-print age that elite consisted mainly of religious scholars.[5] Alongside this religious literature, the indigenous culture of the Turks nurtured a parallel oral tradition that perpetuated historical memory, celebrated collective wisdom, and preserved popular cultural values. Without writing, however, this tradition could not be known to outsiders.

In seventh-century Arabia, a new prophet had appeared, calling tribesmen and townspeople around Mecca and Medina to a new faith—a religion that recognized much of the older biblical teaching but aimed to restore a purity of belief. By the ninth century CE, armies of Arabs and other recent Muslim converts had spread across Iran and deep into Central Asia.[6]

Last on the scene of the great world religions, Islam was always a strongly proselytizing faith. Such missionary activity undoubtedly won some Turkish converts as early as the eighth century. But Islam's most dramatic success in Turkish Central Asia was probably the conversion, in the middle of the tenth century, of the ruler of a confederation of Turkish tribes known collectively as the Karakhanids, and with him "two hundred thousand tents."[7] While the older religions gradually lost adherents in Central Asia, Islam spread rapidly. And with it, Turkish influence in the Muslim world grew. Turkish manpower undergirded several dynasties, Turkish and non-Turkish alike, in the ensuing centuries.

The conversion of a tribal or confederation leader like the just-mentioned Karakhanid ruler would initially have been followed by at least superficial education in the precepts of the new faith. In the case of Islam, this would likely have involved instruction in the Qur'an, stories about the life of the Prophet Muhammad, and basic principles of religious practice: obligatory rituals of prayer and the profession of faith.

From a purely linguistic point of view, the complexity of this project becomes obvious once it is recalled that Islam's foundational text was preserved in Arabic, a Semitic language very different from Altaic Old Turkic. In the instruction of a convert, memorization of important phrases would have been essential; explanation of the Qur'an must have been accompanied by translations or paraphrases. Progress would have been slow. Surviving manuscript copies of "bilingual" Qur'ans (and Qur'an commentaries)—with Turkish phrases translating the Arabic text word for word added interlinearly (or inserted directly into the text)—show how one part of this religious instruction may have been carried out, at least at the level of the ruler's court.[8]

Following the conversion of a politically powerful figure, it is likely that itinerant preachers would have pressed their missionary activity further afield among nomadic tribespeople and settled communities alike. The ruler's adoption of a new faith would have resulted in the extension of an umbrella of protection, so to speak, for religious enthusiasts to spread their teaching even further. Over time, a figurative two-way street emerged: in one direction proselytizers pushing further and further out from older, settled centers; in the other, newly converted Turks becoming ever more fully absorbed into the culture of the new religion, pursuing more formal education in newly established Muslim colleges *(medrese)*. In that process of acculturation, the primary language of learning and communication would not have been Turkish. But conversion to Islam meant that as they became literate, Turks by and large would come to write their language in the Arabic script.

The steppe culture, whose vitality supported more sedentary regimes, would have remained largely unknown to us were it not for an extraordinary book, *The Compendium of Turkish Dialects*. Compiled in 1077 by Mahmud al-Kashgari, a scholar from a princely Karakhanid family, it is an encyclopaedic dictionary written in Arabic. Through its examples of word usage, it gives us a tantalizing view into that culture of Central Asian nomadic Turkish life. Not itself a literary text, the *Compendium* offers a picture of the essentially pre-Islamic oral culture of Turkish Central Asia. It contains a sampling of Turkish proverbs, sayings, and poetry on a variety of subjects from raiding and war to the celebration of nature. The *Compendium* is a unique time capsule from the late eleventh century.[9]

Kashgari's *Compendium* demonstrates precisely, though incidentally and less often remarked upon, the degree of linguistic sophistication that many Turks by then had achieved.[10] The most comprehensive and ambitious work of its time pertaining to Turkish culture, Kashgari's *Compendium* was followed by many other lesser dictionaries, grammars, and glossaries by less well-known authors. While none of them possess the extraordinary interest of Kashgari's work, taken together they witness the continuing rise to prestige and power of Turks throughout the Islamic world.

And it is precisely that political reality—the Turks' rise to prominence in the Islamic Middle East and Central Asia—to which Muslim Turkish literature owes its true beginnings. Convinced of the importance of his native language, Kashgari presented his massive work to the Abbasid caliph, al-Muqtadi, in Baghdad with the aim of introducing and explaining the languages and customs of the Turkic peoples. Whether that objective was realistic is perhaps a moot point. There is a certain poetic justice, however, in the situation: the Arab caliph being asked to better understand the languages and culture of a mostly distant people on whose numbers his own position partly relied. (The political dynasty that then supported the caliph in Baghdad was that of the Seljuks, a family belonging to the larger grouping of Oghuz Turks.)

Shortly before Kashgari compiled his dictionary, another Central Asian Turk, Yusuf of Balasaghun, had composed, in 1069, a long didactic poem of the "mirror-for-princes" genre that he presented to the Karakhanid ruler, Bughra Khan, in Kashgar. Scholars have accorded Yusuf's *Kutadgu Bilig* ("Wisdom of the Royal Glory") the honor of "first work of Muslim Turkish literature." (The language of the poem is classified as "Middle Turkic.") Given the length and sophistication of Yusuf's poem, really a treatise on political philosophy, it seems likely that it was not the first book set down by a Muslim Turk in his own language. Other, less ambitious works must have preceded Yusuf's, but being of less distinction they have not survived.[11]

Nevertheless, the subject matter of Yusuf's poem is fitting for that honor of primacy of place. In his poem, Yusuf "aimed to show that the Turkish traditions of royalty and wisdom were comparable or superior to their Arab and Iranian counterparts, and were equally compatible with Islam." So where Kashgari produced a scholarly volume that rationalized the study of Turkish traditions and the use of Turkish languages, Yusuf produced a work in his own language to provide his Turkish-speaking patron with a suitable guide to conduct.[12]

Mahmud Kashgari almost certainly never visited Anatolia, but the picture he presents of indigenous Oghuz Turkish culture in Central Asia equally reflects the ethos of the Seljuk Turks' westernmost province. After all, Oghuz tribesmen were prominent among the armies that won a key victory in 1071 (Battle of Manzikert), which opened the way to Turkish colonization of Anatolia and the establishment of the "Rum" Seljuk state with its capital in Konya.[13]

Kashgari had no Anatolian counterpart, but a work of comparable importance to his *Compendium* has survived: "The Book of Dede Korkut" *(Kitab-i Dede Korkut)*. This anonymous collection of a dozen heroic tales, narrated in a mixture of Turkish "prose" and verse, vividly reveals the oral culture that must have prevailed among Turkish tribes in Anatolia in Seljuk times. It is a vibrant culture, only lightly Islamized. With their extended narratives and compelling plots, the stories in the "Book of Dede Korkut" constitute a unique counterpart to Kashgari's collection of verse fragments, pithy sayings, and proverbial wisdom from Central Asia.[14]

We do not know the circumstances of the writing down of the Dede Korkut collection—the stories are a good deal older than the probable sixteenth-century date of the surviving manuscripts—nor for whom they were intended; only that the storyteller from time to time addresses "my khan," the notable in whose presence the tales were narrated. Preserved in two rather different manuscript copies, these stories were clearly intended for oral delivery or "performance." The teller of the tales intermittently accompanies himself on a stringed instrument while switching from one declamatory register to another. The tales are rooted in an oral storytelling tradition of considerable age and maturity. (And popular oral storytelling, celebrating the deeds of brigand heroes and the lives of star-crossed lovers, continued to thrive for centuries in Anatolia.[15]) An even more evolved tradition of oral epic may well have existed then among Turkish speakers, but it is only attested at a much later date.[16]

From the late eleventh century on, Anatolia was a patchwork of ethnicities. The Anatolian Seljuk sultans, essentially independent of the more powerful dynasty of the same family name in Iraq, ruled over a countryside where the majority religion (Orthodox Christianity) and language (principally Greek but also Armenian) were different from their own. They also exercised, at best, nominal authority over large numbers of those Turkish horsemen and herders who had initially helped bring them to power but who were disinclined to respect their urban overlords. However that may be, the culture that Seljuk rulers and their chief statesmen patronized in Konya and other major Anatolian cities for nearly two centuries was an extension of the sophisticated cosmopolitan world of Baghdad and other old Islamic centers—if on a smaller scale. In Konya and elsewhere in the Seljuk domain, the language of learning and administration was principally Arabic; of literature, Persian. Turkish in "Turkey" was not yet a written language.

It was Konya where Jalaladdin Rumi lived most of his life, composing a vast body of mystic poetry, a poetry almost entirely in Persian.[17] Soon after Rumi's death (in 1273), a circle of followers, including his son, established a mystical "order" (*tarikat*), the Mevlevi, which helped perpetuate Rumi's creative output, maintained a powerful presence in Konya, and spread a sophisticated blend of spirituality and music that exercised enormous influence in the later Ottoman Empire, especially in its capitol, Istanbul. (The order continues to exist today.)[18] But the gulf between Rumi's Persian poetry—and the spirit that informed it—and the Turkish Dede Korkut tales is enormous. Those two collections animate and illuminate two vastly different worlds.

Whether Kashgari's dedicatee, the Abbasid caliph in Baghdad, went on to study Turkish seems doubtful. But the Turks' rise to power in the Muslim world did create a demand for translations (or reworkings) of older books written in Persian and Arabic. If a Turkish prince (*han, beg,* or *sultan*) had a modest excuse for not being able to read Arabic or Persian classics, it was increasingly inexcusable that he not be familiar with paraphrases of those works in Turkish. Would-be authors might be rewarded for their efforts in helping that enterprise along. But apart from their political accomplishments and a modest record of civic building (mainly in the form of caravansaries), the Anatolian Seljuk ruling class seems to have been too busy securing its rather precarious position to have taken on the task of patronizing a new literature in the Turkish language.[19]

That task would fall to other patrons—local Turkish (or Turkoman) chiefs who rose to power and eventually established petty courts in several smaller Anatolian cities in the decentralized political climate that followed in the wake of the Mongol deluge and the disappearance of the Seljuk dynasty. It was at the courts of those chiefs (*begs*) in the late thirteenth century that Anatolian Turkish authors, writing in their own language, began to appear. Those petty rulers, whose names are now largely forgotten, became the patrons of a historic first generation of aspiring authors. Whether there had been earlier efforts in this direction we will probably never know. For now we can say that it was during that *beylik* period that the young tree of Turkish literary creativity finally bore fruit.

By the end of the fourteenth century, there was a substantial harvest. As one scholar recently put it, this harvest amounted to "a momentous literary event . . . the emergence of the Islamic Western Turkish literature at all cultural levels, folk, popular and elite."[20] That harvest included adaptations of romances and stories written in Persian or Arabic and age-old wisdom literature originating in India. It included works in both prose and verse. "Tales of the Prophets" were among them. Most impressive perhaps was a collection of mystic poetry by Yunus Emre, influenced by Rumi but of powerfully original inspiration.[21] Hamza's "Story of Joseph" is another fruit from that same harvest. Inspired by religious enthusiasm and shaped by oral storytelling practice, his poem links two imaginative worlds.

The shadowy practice of professional sheyyad storytelling perhaps outlived Hamza's time but it disappeared shortly thereafter. It left little evidence behind of its poorly known performance tradition. As religion became increasingly institutionalized, popular preaching may have moved from the public square into the mosque. And as the Ottoman *beylik* expanded into a world empire ruled from Istanbul, an urban elite fostered a sophisticated literature patronized by the well-to-do.[22] Much else survived as well, but survival depended on popularity or luck.

However one judges Hamza's poem—and scholars of Turkish literature have credited it more for its antiquity than for any perceived artistry—the "Story of Joseph" survives as a persuasive witness to its time, a striking example of one way in which an inspired preacher-poet might have proselytized for Islam.

Notes

1. For linguistic overview of the several languages, see Lars Johanson and Eva Csato, eds., *The Turkic Languages* (New York: Routledge, 1998).

2. For centuries unknown to the outside world, the stones were discovered, deciphered, and published only in the late nineteenth century. For the translation of one inscription ("Kul Tigin"), by K. Oztopcu and Seth-Williams, with a sample of the runic text, see Kemal Silay, ed., *An Anthology of Turkish Literature* (Bloomington: Indiana University, 1996), 1–10. For a photograph of the stele with Tonyukuk inscription, see Carter V. Findley, *The Turks in World History* (New York: Oxford University Press, 2005) 42.

3. Hamza would not have been able to read the inscriptions on those stones, or even understand their Turkic texts if he had.

4. For the Inner Asian background, see Svat Soucek, *A History of Inner Asia* (New York: Cambridge University Press, 2000), or Findley, *The Turks in World History.*

5. For translations by L. Clark of two Turkic Manichean poems: Silay, *An Anthology of Turkish Literature,* 11–12. A larger sampling from the same material is given by Hans-Joachim Klimkeit, *Gnosis on the Silk Road: Gnostic Texts from Central Asia* (San Francisco: Harper San Francisco, 1993).

6. For an overview of Arabia, Muhammad, and the spread of Islam: Albert Hourani, *A History of the Arab Peoples* (Cambridge: Harvard University Press, 1991).

7. Findley, *The Turks in World History,* 75, quoting an unnamed source.

8. Several of these bilingual Qur'ans have been published, primarily for their linguistic value. For an overview, see Eleazar Birnbaum, "On Some Turkish Interlinear Translations of the Koran," *Journal of Turkish Studies* 14 (1990): 113–38.

9. For the meticulously translated and annotated text, see Robert Dankoff and James Kelly, trans., *Compendium of the Turkic Dialects* (Türk Şiveleri Lügati [Divanü Lugat-it-Türk]), 3 vols., Sources of Oriental Languages and Literatures (Duxbury, MA: Harvard University Printing Office, 1982–85), 7.

10. Kashgari's book reveals the author's intimate knowledge of Arabic, its grammar, and much else as well of a traditional Islamic education.

11. For a translation of this work with helpful introduction and comment, see Robert Dankoff, trans., *Wisdom of Royal Glory (Kutadgu Bilig) [by] Yusuf Khass Hajib* (Chicago: University of Chicago Press, 1983). Balasaghun, a now lost city, is to be sought in today's Kirghiz Republic.

12. Dankoff, *Wisdom*, 1.

13. For "Rum," see introduction, n. 46.

14. See Geoffrey Lewis's translation, *The Book of Dede Korkut* (Harmondsworth, U.K.: Penguin, 1974), and the introduction to this volume.

15. For the Turkish *aşık* tradition of oral narrative, see İlhan Başgöz, *Hikaye: Turkish Folk Romance as Performance Art* (Bloomington: Indiana University Press, 2008).

16. Epic narratives of truly Homeric scale, documented and recorded in the nineteenth century from some Central Asian Turkic sources, offer an idea of what such traditions might have looked like. Whether those in fact flourished five hundred to a thousand years earlier is by no means certain. For translations of oral (sometimes epic) poetry from Kirgiz, Uzbek, Kazakh, and Altai Turkic languages, see, respectively, Arthur T. Hatto, *The Memorial Feast for Kökötöy-khan (Kökötöydün aši)*, London Oriental Series, vol. 33 (Oxford: Oxford University Press, 1977); Karl Reichl, *Singing the Past* (Ithaca: Cornell University Press, 2000); Thomas G. Winner, *The Oral Art and Literature of the Kazakhs of Russian Central Asia* (Durham: Duke University Press, 1958); and Norman Cohn, *Gold Khan* (London: Secker and Warburg, 1946). For a broad overview, see Nora K. Chadwick and Victor Zhirmunsky, *Oral Epics of Central Asia* (London: Cambridge University Press, 1969).

17. For Rumi's life and poetry: Annemarie Schimmel, *The Triumphal Sun: a Study of the Works of Jalaloddin Rumi* (London: East-West Publications, 1980). Rumi included numerous references to Joseph in his poetry. See Schimmel, "Yusuf in Mawlana Rumi's Poetry," in *The Heritage of Sufism* vol. 2, ed. Leonard Lewisohn (Oxford: One World, 1999), 45–59.

18. For a popular account with evocative illustrations, see Shems Friedlander, *The Whirling Dervishes: Being an Account of the Sufi Order Known as*

the Mevlevis and Its Founder the Poet and Mystic Mevlana Jalalu'ddin Rumi (Albany: State University of New York Press, 1992).

19. For Seljuk-era buildings: Oktay Aslanapa, *Turkish Art and Architecture* (New York: Praeger, 1971). An insightful overview is presented by Gary Leiser, "Research on the Seljuks of Anatolia: Some Comments on the State of the Art" in A.C.S. Peacock and Sara Nur Yildiz, eds., *The Seljuks of Anatolia: Court and Society in the Medieval Middle East* (London: Tauris, 2013), 264–75.

20. A. T. Karamustafa, writing on "Early Turkish Islamic Literature up to the Ottomans," *EI2*, x, 716.

21. See Smith, *The Poetry of Yunus Emre.*

22. For examples of a mature Ottoman Turkish literature, see Walter G. Andrews et al., eds., *Ottoman Lyric Poetry: An Anthology*, expanded ed. (Seattle: University of Washington Press, 2006); and Victoria Rowe Holbrook, ed., *Seyh Galip, Beauty and Love* (New York: Modern Language Association of America, 2005).

Synopsis

Any synopsis must be arbitrary and selective, and what follows is no exception. I have singled out what seem to me notable scene markers and motifs. Many extend through more than a single verse of the poem. My identification is by the number of the line (following the recent Istanbul editions) where the scene begins.

0001. Opening
0018. Jacob's family, in Canaan
0021. Joseph's dream
0046. Jacob's dream
0057. Joseph's brothers plot his murder
0101. Joseph is dropped into the well
0104. Gabriel intervenes; prevents Joseph's death
0108. Hud and the story of the well
0126. Gabriel's reappearance
0140. The brothers' story of the wolf
0165. The Egyptian merchant and his dream
0191. Joseph looks in the mirror

0197. Joseph is rescued
0211. The negotiated sale of Joseph
0235. The merchant's caravan sets off for Egypt
0236. At Rachel's grave; the storm
0257. The caravan arrives at Banyas
0269. In Jerusalem: the king and his dream
0290. The caravan reaches Arish
0301. Arrival in Egypt; Joseph is put on display; Joseph bathes
0326. Zeliha is introduced; her dreams
0351. Taymus writes to the ruler of Egypt
0387. Qutayfar purchases Joseph
0394. Joseph reveals his identity to the merchant
0426. Zeliha's love of Joseph
0437. The destruction of Zeliha's idols
0452. Zeliha's nurse and her advice; Zeliha builds a palace
0478. Zeliha has a palace built
0481. Zeliha's attempted seduction of Joseph
0512. First "moral"
0548. Qutayfar discovers Zeliha and Joseph; Zeliha's false accusation
0559. The infant exonerates Joseph
0569. The women of Egypt
0590. They cut their hands
0607. Joseph is thrown in prison

0609. Death of Qutayfar; succeeded by his brother, Reyyan

0612. Gabriel visits Joseph: Joseph will achieve power and prosperity

0617. Story of Caesar and the plot to poison Reyyan

0625. The cupbearer's and the steward's dreams; Joseph's interpretations

0647. Gabriel questions Joseph

0662. The Arab merchant; his visit to Jacob

0701. Gabriel visits Joseph again

0705. The Egyptian king's dream

0726. Joseph interprets the king's dream

0744. Zeliha confesses her love for Joseph

0756. Joseph is released from prison; Gabriel visits again

0760. Second "moral"

0820. Joseph intercedes for those in prison

0827. The years of plenty, followed by drought

0844. Third "moral"

0857. Joseph's marvelous horse

0864. Gabriel reprimands Joseph

0869. Zeliha's destitution

0907. Zeliha's youth and beauty are restored; she and Joseph are wed

0924. Joseph constructs a network of roads

0930. Fourth "moral"

0946. Famine in Canaan; Jacob sends his sons to Egypt

0964. Joseph summons his brothers to his palace
0996. Joseph's brothers return to Jacob
1023. The brothers return to Egypt, now bringing Benjamin
1028. Gabriel announces their arrival to Joseph
1033. Joseph goes in disguise to rescue Jacob
1060. Joseph has another palace built with pictures of his father and brothers
1091. Joseph reveals his identity to Benjamin
1131. Joseph feasts his brothers; he sits with Benjamin
1138. Joseph conceals Benjamin's cup in his brothers' sack; Benjamin is detained as a thief
1152. A story of Joseph's childhood and theft of a gem
1170. Joseph has Benjamin put in prison
1175. The brothers attempt to oppose Joseph and rescue Benjamin
1199. Joseph sends the brothers back again to Jacob
1212. The Angel of Death appears to Jacob: "Your son is alive"
1242. Jacob writes a letter to the King of Egypt; the brothers return to Joseph with the letter
1265. Joseph confronts his brothers with the contract of his sale
1281. Joseph questions the magic cup
1293. The brothers accept the cup's responses
1309. Joseph reveals himself to his brothers; they ask for forgiveness

1314. Joseph's brothers see his face
1321. Joseph pardons his brothers
1327. Why Joseph sends his shirt to Jacob; the story of Jacob's concubine (Joseph's wet nurse) and Jacob's heartless sale of her son
1345. Joseph sends his shirt and a letter back to Jacob with his servant, Beshir
1373. Beshir is reunited with his mother, Jacob's former concubine
1388. Jacob reads Joseph's reply
1395. Joseph sends his brothers back to Canaan; they confess their guilt to Jacob who pardons them
1403. Gabriel tells Jacob to go to Egypt
1416. Fifth "moral"
1438. Zeliha and Joseph build a house for Jacob
1448. Gabriel tells Jacob to return to Canaan
1457. Jacob dies; his sons bury him
1476. Gabriel announces Joseph's prophethood to him; Joseph calls the Egyptians to the true faith; he destroys their churches
1482. Joseph and his brothers move out of the city and found a new one
1495. The king of Egypt accepts Joseph's religion
1500. Zeliha dies, followed by Joseph
1504. The placement of Joseph's coffin is a source of dispute; it is put in the middle of the river

1514. God commands Moses to remove the coffin from the river

1524. The poet ends his story

Bibliography

Alter, Robert. *Genesis: Translation and Commentary.* New York: W. W. Norton, 1996.

And, Metin. *A History of Theatre and Popular Entertainment in Turkey.* Ankara: Forum, 1963.

Andrews, Walter G., et al. *Ottoman Lyric Poetry: An Anthology.* Expanded edition. Seattle: University of Washington Press, 2006.

Aslanapa, Oktay. *Turkish Art and Architecture.* New York: Praeger, 1971.

Attar, Farid al-din. *The Ilahi-nama; or, Book of God.* Translated by John Andrew Boyle. Manchester: Manchester University Press, 1976.

Barry, Michael A. *Figurative Art in Medieval Islam and the Riddle of Bihzad of Herat (1465–1535).* New York: Rizzoli, 2004.

Başgöz, Ilhan. *Hikaye: Turkish Folk Romance as Performance Art.* Bloomington: Indiana University Press, 2008.

Beeston, A.F.L. *Baidawi's Commentary on Surah 12 of the Qur'an.* Oxford: Oxford University Press, 1963.

———. "Notes on a Middle Arabic 'Joseph' Poem," *Bulletin of the School of Oriental and African Studies* [London University] 40 (1977): 287–96.

Birnbaum, Eleazar. "On Some Turkish Interlinear Translations of the Koran." *Journal of Turkish Studies* 14 (1990): 113–38.

Blum, Pamela Z. "The Middle English Romance 'Iacob and Iosep' and the Joseph Cycle of the Salisbury Chapter House." *Gesta* 8 (1969): 18–34.

Boeschoten, H. E., and J. O'Kane and M. Vandamme, trans. *Al-Rabghuzi: The Stories of the Prophets*, vol. 2. Leiden: Brill, 1995.

Brinner, William M., trans. *"Ara'is al-Majalis fi Qisas al-Anbiya," or "Lives of the Prophets."* Boston: Brill, 2002.

Chadwick, Nora K., and Victor Zhirmunsky. *Oral Epics of Central Asia*. London: Cambridge University Press, 1969.

Cohn, Norman. *Gold Khan*. London: Secker and Warburg, 1946.

Dankoff, Robert. *Wisdom of Royal Glory: A Turko-Islamic Mirror for Princes*. Chicago: University of Chicago Press, 1983.

Dankoff, Robert, and James Kelly. *Compendium of the Turkic Dialects / Türk Şiveleri Lügati (Divanü Lugat-it-Turk)*. 3 vols. Sources of Oriental Languages and Literatures, 7. Duxbury, MA: Harvard University Printing Office, 1982–85.

Dunn, Ross E. *The Adventures of Ibn Battuta*. Berkeley: University of California Press, 1986.

Ebied, R. Y., and M.J.L. Young. *The Story of Joseph in Arabic Verse: The Leeds Arabic Manuscript 347*. Annual of Leeds Oriental Society, supplement 3. Leiden: Brill, 1975.

Elsie, Robert. *History of Albanian Literature*. Vol. 1. Boulder, CO: Social Science Monographs, 1995.

Encyclopaedia Judaica. Second edition, 22 vols. New York: Thomson Gale, 2007.

Encyclopaedia of Islam. New edition, 12 vols. Leiden: Brill, 1979–2004.

Encyclopaedia of the Qur'an. 5 vols. Boston: Brill, 2001–6.

Esin, Emel. *Turkish Miniature Painting*. Rutland, VT: Charles E. Tuttle, 1960.

Findley, Carter V. *The Turks in World History*. New York: Oxford University Press, 2005.

Friedlander, Shems. *The Whirling Dervishes: Being an Account of the Sufi Order Known as the Mevlevis and Its Founder the Poet and Mystic Mevlana Jalalu'ddin Rumi*. Albany: State University of New York Press, 1992.

Gibb, Elias John Wilkinson. *A History of Ottoman Poetry*. Vol. 2. Edited by E. G. Browne. London: Luzac, 1902.

Gibb, Hamilton A. R. *Travels of Ibn Battuta, A.D. 1325–1354*. 4 vols. Hakluyt Society 2nd series. Cambridge, U.K.: Cambridge University Press, 1958–2000.

Ginzberg, Louis. *The Legends of the Jews*. 2 vols. Translated by Henrietta Szold. Baltimore: Johns Hopkins University Press, 1998.

Hatto, Arthur T. *The Memorial Feast for Kökötöy-Khan*. London Oriental Series, 33. Oxford: Oxford University Press, 1977.

Hickman, Bill. "From Oral Story to Literary Text: Rethinking an Old Ottoman Poem." Festschrift in Honor of Andras J. E. Bodrogligeti. *Türk Dilleri Araştırmaları* 17 (2007): 177–89.

———. "Notes on a Fourteenth-Century Anatolian Turkish Poem." In *Puzzles of Language: Essays in Honour of Karl Zimmer*, 227–34. Edited by Eser Erguvanlı Taylan and Bengisu Rona. Turcologica, 86. Wiesbaden: Harrassowitz, 2011.

———. "On Listening to Şeyyad Hamza's 'Destan-i Yusuf.'" *Turkish Studies Association Journal* 29 (2005), 65–73.

———. "Reflections on Şeyyad Hamza's *Story of Joseph*: Apropos Two Recent Publications." *Journal of Turkish Literature* [Ankara] 9 (2012): 9–29.

Holbrook, Victoria Rowe, trans. *Şeyh Galip, Beauty and Love*. New York: Modern Language Association of America, 2005.

Hollis, Susan. *The Ancient Egyptian "Tale of Two Brothers,"* 2nd ed. Oakville, CT: Bannerstone Press, 2008.

Hourani, Albert. *A History of the Arab Peoples*. Cambridge: Harvard University Press, 1991.

Isaac, E. "The Ethiopic History of Joseph." *Journal for the Study of the Pseudepigrapha* 6 (1990): 3–125.

Jarring, Gunnar, ed., and trans. *Literary Texts from Kashgar*. Lund: CWK Gleerup, 1980. Acta Regiae Societatis Humaniorum Litterarum Lundensis 74.

Jeffrey, Arthur. *A Reader on Islam*. 'S-Gravenhage: Mouton, 1962.

Johanson, Lars, and Eva Csato, eds. *The Turkic Languages*. New York: Routledge, 1998.

Johns, Anthony H. "Joseph in the Qur'an: Dramatic Dialogue, Human Emotion, and Prophetic Wisdom." *Islamochristiana* 7 (1981): 29–55.

Klimkeit, Hans-Joachim. *Gnosis on the Silk Road: Gnostic Texts from Central Asia*. San Francisco: Harper, 1993.

Knappert, Jan. *Islamic Legends: Histories of the Heroes, Saints, and Prophets of Islam*. Leiden: Brill, 1985.

Kraemer, Ross Shepard. *When Aseneth Met Joseph*. New York: Oxford University Press, 1998.

Kugel, James L. *In Potiphar's House: The Interpretive Life of Biblical Tales*. New York: Harper, 1990.

Lamoreaux, John C. *The Early Muslim Tradition of Dream Interpretation*. Albany: State University of New York Press, 2002.

Leiser, Gary. "Research on the Seljuks of Anatolia: Some Comments on the State of the Art." In *The Seljuks of Anatolia: Court and Society in the Medieval Middle East*, edited by A.C.S. Peacock and Sara Nur Yıldız. London: Tauris, 2013.

Lewis, Geoffrey. *The Book of Dede Korkut*. Harmondsworth, U.K.: Penguin, 1974.

Lord Raglan. "The Hero of Tradition." In *The Myth and Ritual Theory: An Anthology*, edited by Robert A. Segal. Malden, MA: Blackwell, 1998.

Mahallati, Mohammad J. "The Significance of Dreams and Dream Interpretation in the Qur'an: Two Sufi Commentaries on Surat

Yusuf." In *Dreaming across Boundaries: The Interpetation of Dreams in Islamic Lands*, edited by Louise Marlow. Boston: Ilex Foundation, 2008.

Martinovitch, Nicholas N. *The Turkish Theatre*. 1933. Reprint; New York: Blom, 1968.

McGaha, Michael. *Coat of Many Cultures*. Philadelphia: Jewish Publication Society, 1997.

Meri, Josef W., trans. *A Lonely Wayfarer's Guide to Pilgrimage*. Princeton: Darwin Press, 2004.

Metropolitan Museum of Art. *Venice and the Islamic World 828–1797*. New Haven: Yale University Press, 2007.

Milstein, Rachel, et al. *Stories of the Prophets: Illustrated Manuscripts of "Qisas al-Anbiya."* Costa Mesa, CA: Mazda, 1999.

Moreen, Vera Basch. *In Queen Esther's Garden: An Anthology of Judeo-Persian Literature*. New Haven: Yale University Press, 2000.

Napier, Arthur S. *Iacob and Iosep: A Middle English Poem of the Thirteenth Century*. London: Oxford University Press, 1916.

Noegel, Scott B., and Brannon M. Wheeler. *Historical Dictionary of Prophets in Islam and Judaism*. Lanham, MD: Scarecrow, 2002.

Pendlebury, David, trans. *Yusuf and Zulaikha: An Allegorical Romance by Hakim Nuruddin Abdurrahman Jami*. London: Octagon Press, 1980.

Pickthall, Marmaduke. *The Meaning of the Glorious Koran*. 1930. New York: New American Library, 1953.

Reichl, Karl. *Singing the Past*. Ithaca: Cornell University Press, 2000.

Ricklefs, M. C. *The Seen and Unseen Worlds in Java, 1726–1749*. Honolulu: University of Hawai'i Press, 1998.

Ritter, Helmut. *The Ocean of the Soul*. Translated by John O'Kane. Boston: Brill, 2003.

Schimmel, Annemarie. *The Triumphal Sun: A Study of the Works of Jalaloddin Rumi*. London: East-West Publications, 1980.

Seguy, Marie-Rose. *The Miraculous Journey of Mahomet: Miraj Nameh.* Translated by R. Pevear. New York: G. Braziller, 1977.

Silay, Kemal, ed. *An Anthology of Turkish Literature.* Bloomington: Indiana University, 1996.

Smith, Grace Martin. *The Poetry of Yunus Emre, a Turkish Sufi Poet.* Berkeley: University of California Press, 1993.

———. *Yusuf-i Meddah, Varqa ve Gulsah.* Leiden: Brill, 1976.

Soucek, Svat. *A History of Inner Asia.* New York: Cambridge University Press, 2000.

Thackston, W. M. "The Paris Mi'rajnama." *Journal of Turkish Studies* 18 (1994): 263–85.

Thackston, W. M., Jr., trans. *The Tales of the Prophets of al-Kisa'i.* Boston: Twayne, 1978.

Weitzmann, Kurt, and Herbert L. Kessler. *The Cotton Genesis: British Library Codex Cotton Otho B. VI.* Princeton: Princeton University Press, 1986.

Wellesz, Emmy. *The Vienna Genesis.* London: Faber and Faber, 1960.

West, Steven L. "The First Story of Joseph in Turkic Islamic Literature." PhD diss., UCLA, 1975.

Winner, Thomas G. *The Oral Art and Literature of the Kazakhs of Russian Central Asia.* Durham: Duke University Press, 1958.

Yohannan, John D. *Joseph and Potiphar's Wife in World Literature.* New York: New Directions, 1968.